Praise for *Live Your Calling*

"What you do with your life deeply [impacts] [...] [this] work is a gift to those who are searching and to thos[e] [who] [help] [light] the way."

—Tim Clinton, president,
American Association of Christian Counselors

"A wonderful book that helps us discover, from a spiritual and natural gifting perspective, God's unique purpose for our life. Every person needs to know why God made them. This book will help you move toward a greater understanding of this."

—Os Hillman, president, Marketplace Leaders
and the International Coalition of Workplace Ministries

"Here is a superb road map for understanding your potential, finding God's will, and investing your life productively for Christ. I highly recommend this book."

—M. Blaine Smith, director, Nehemiah Ministries;
author, *Knowing God's Will*

"In a world too often marked by transience and a sense of 'getting by,'" this book presents a challenging alternative. It clarifies the exciting possibilities of understanding your purpose and lays out very practical steps to fulfilling your calling."

—Robby Richardson, director, Internet Ministries,
Gospel Communications International

"The tools and principles in this book can help young adults get their bearings and conquer obstacles."

—Rebecca Horst, director, CALL Project, Goshen College

"A practical exercise in understanding your unique calling, stretching your God-sized vision, and living it out where God has placed you. These tools help you maximize your effectiveness in your workplace and in every part of your life."

—Kent Humphreys, president, Fellowship of
Companies for Christ International

"The Brennflecks uniquely and strategically provide an interactive process to identify, explore, experience, and confirm our personal giftedness, which enhances our sense of individual destiny and worth, resulting in deep feelings of personal fulfillment."

—Dr. Gordon E. Kirk, senior pastor, Lake Ave. Church

"I enthusiastically recommend this to anyone questioning the calling of their life. I believe each of us have been gifted by God to lean into the gifts and abilities he has given us. The purpose of your life is out there to be discovered. This book and the tools provided by Kevin and Kay Marie Brennfleck can be a road map to make that discovery. I highly recommend it to you."

—Jon Wallace, president, Azusa Pacific University

"This book reflects sensitive, careful, and practical thinking about the nature of God's call. It is the ideal handbook for churches, organizations, and small groups serious about discipleship and helping people find their callings and live their dreams for the kingdom of God. For any one searching for a way to serve and to make a difference in the world, this ought to be the next book on your reading list."

—Philip Carlson, family physician; senior pastor, Bethany Church

Live Your Calling

A Practical Guide to Finding and Fulfilling Your Mission in Life

Kevin and Kay Marie Brennfleck

JOSSEY-BASS
A Wiley Imprint
www.josseybass.com

Published by Jossey-Bass
A Wiley Imprint
989 Market Street, San Francisco, CA 94103-1741   www.josseybass.com

Jossey-Bass books and products are available through most bookstores. To contact Jossey-Bass directly call
our Customer Care Department within the U.S. at 800-956-7739, outside the U.S. at 317-572-399386, or
fax 317-572-4002.

Jossey-Bass also publishes its books in a variety of electronic formats. Some content that appears in print
may not be available in electronic books.

The publisher and the author make no representations or warranties with respect to the accuracy or com-
pleteness of the contents of this work and specifically disclaim all warranties, including without limitation
warranties of fitness for a particular purpose. No warranty may be created or extended by sales or promo-
tional materials. The advice and strategies contained herein may not be suitable for every situation. This
work is sold with the understanding that the publisher is not engaged in rendering legal, accounting, or other
professional services. If professional assistance is required, the services of a competent professional person
should be sought. Neither the publisher nor the author shall be liable for damages arising herefrom. The fact
that an organization or Website is referred to in this work as a citation and/or a potential source of further
information does not mean that the author or the publisher endorses the information the organization or
Website may provide or recommendations it may make. Further, readers should be aware that Internet Websites listed in this work may have changed or disappeared between when this work was written and when it is
read. In some cases, the identity and all identifiable details of persons described have been disguised.

"Life Calling Map" United States trademark registration by Kevin and Kay Marie Brennfleck.

All scripture quotations, unless otherwise indicated, are taken from the HOLY BIBLE, NEW INTERNA-
TIONAL VERSION®. NIV®. Copyright ©1973, 1978, 1984 by International Bible Society. Used by permission of Zondervan. All rights reserved.

Library of Congress Cataloging-in-Publication Data

Brennfleck, Kevin, date.
Live your calling: a practical guide to finding and fulfilling your mission in life /
Kevin and Kay Marie Brennfleck.—1st ed.
    p. cm.
  Includes bibliographical references.
  ISBN 0–7879–6895–1 (alk. paper)
  1. Vocation—Christianity. I. Brennfleck, Kay Marie, date. II. Title.
  BV4740.B74 2004
  248.4—dc22   2004014551

Printed in the United States of America
FIRST EDITION
PB Printing 10 9 8 7 6 5 4 3 2

CONTENTS

To our beloved children,
Brian and Amy,
who bring us much joy

May you always
"walk worthy"
of the calling
you have received

INTRODUCTION

A FedEx commercial parodied the movie *Cast Away*, in which Tom Hanks played a FedEx worker whose company plane went down, stranding him on a remote island for years. Looking like the bedraggled Hanks from the movie, the FedEx employee in the commercial walks up to the door of a home, holding a package.

When a woman comes to the door, he explains that he survived five years on an island, protecting this package in order to deliver it to her. Curious, he asks her to reveal what is in it. Opening the package and displaying the contents, the woman replies that there was nothing of great importance; just a GPS navigational device, a compass, a satellite telephone, a water purifier, and assorted seeds.

Most of us experience times when we feel lost or as though we are just surviving in life. Sometimes we feel disoriented by the circumstances and decisions we face. As young adults, we have to choose a career direction for the first time. Later in life we may have to do so again as the result of midlife changes, job loss, the empty nest, divorce, a spiritual awakening, or retirement. *What should I do? Which way should I go?* we wonder.

Other times we may look at the familiar routine of our days, weeks, and years and be struck by a sense of purposelessness. We fear that we are experiencing but a shadow of the life we were meant to live. In the quiet places of our soul we hear whispered, "There's got to be more to life than this."

When we query the purpose and direction of our lives, we are asking questions about our calling. Your calling is an invitation to live the life you are meant to live. You are called to become the person you were created to be and do the things you were designed to do. As you live your calling, you will find the purpose for which you were born.

As with the contents of the FedEx package, the resources you need are right at hand within this book. It contains effective tools for you to use within your unique life situation. Whether you currently are in school, working, at home with children, or retired, this book gives you a road map and the resources needed for finding and fulfilling your mission in life.

We write this book both as fellow travelers and as guides in the search to discover one's purpose in life. For many years we have had the privilege of serving as career counselors, life calling coaches, and seminar leaders to thousands of men and women. We are grateful to our clients for inviting us into their lives. Trusting us to facilitate their search for work and volunteer activities that use their gifts, they also have looked to us to help them find answers to the larger questions about their purpose, mission, and calling in life. With permission, we have included many of their stories in this book. (Other illustrative examples we use are composites of several people and do not represent specific individuals.)

We believe that we are called to write this book as a travel guide for those who are seeking both spiritual and practical answers to the question, "What is my purpose in life?" We can write authentically only from the context of our own life journey, which is directed and shaped by our commitment to follow Jesus Christ. Throughout this book we draw from the timeless truths found in the Bible, which give reliable and pragmatic instruction for discovering and living an extraordinary life.

Using This Book as a Toolbox to Find Your Calling

We call this book a practical guide because it offers a useful toolbox of principles, assessment exercises, strategies, and other resources that assist you in taking the right action steps to create a life of purpose and passion. In this book you have the opportunity to:

• *Complete six inventories* to identify key dimensions, or "puzzle pieces," of your unique design: your most-enjoyed skills, core values, preferred roles, personality traits, compelling interests, and spiritual gifts. You can record your assessment results in a document called your Life Calling Map. It is an important tool for clarifying your God-given design and discovering your calling within your work, home, church, community, and the world at large.

• *Enlarge your vision of what you can do.* Most people have dreams for their lives that are too small, limited by lack of vision, fear, and everyday concerns. God calls us to undertake tasks and roles we cannot accomplish on our own so that we can see his power at work.

Your Life Calling Map can be used to identify and explore options for work and volunteer ministry/service activities that are in alignment with your God-given design. Using strategies for brainstorming, dreaming big, and investigating possibilities helps you expand your vision of what God is calling you to do in the world.

• *Learn how to make good decisions within God's will for your life.* Your calling doesn't just happen without your participation. Partnering with God to live your calling requires making decisions. Learning to make good decisions about life choices is an essential part of spiritual maturity.

• *Consider emotional, psychological, spiritual, and lifestyle issues that can get you stuck* as you seek to find and fulfill your mission in life. You can assess if any of these "calling blockers" are hindering you in discerning or living your calling. We introduce "calling catalysts" you can use to conquer your personal calling blockers.

• *Motivate yourself to take action.* Learning how to take appropriate action is a key part of becoming a person God can fully use. You will have the opportunity to create personal mission statements, set achievable and compelling goals, and develop an action plan to create the life God is calling you to live.

• *Learn how to live your calling successfully.* Your life matters in God's majestic plan. Many people are inspired to pursue their calling; fewer persevere to live it faithfully over the course of their lives. Tapping into God's power and resources, creating a vital support system, and more fully developing the characteristics of a called person enable you to fulfill the mission that is yours alone.

Prayerful Action Steps

St. Augustine, the fifth-century theologian, said that we should pray as though everything depended on God and work as though everything depended on us. Living your calling requires prayerful action. The sequence of action steps laid out in this book is a proven path on which to walk. To get the most out of this book and to help ensure your success in discovering the life of purpose God desires you to have, we suggest that you do the following:

• Obtain a journal or notebook to record the events of your journey. Your responses to the discussion questions and activities at the end of each chapter create an ongoing account of how God is working in your life, which helps you discern where he is leading you.

• Find one or more companions to share the journey. Look for people who want to work through this book, and create a Live Your Calling Group. One partner is good; a small group of six to eight people is ideal. There is a Live Your Calling Small Group Guide in Appendix A, at the back of the book; it outlines a suggested twelve-week format for going through this book. You and your partner(s) can assist one another with feedback, input, accountability, and encouragement.

Opening the Package

If you were on a desert island like Hanks's character in *Cast Away*, would you leave one package unopened? The desire to keep one package intact as a tangible sign of hope that we will one day get home to deliver it is understandable. For many of us, however, the symbolic value of the package would be outweighed by the potential real-world value of its contents to help us move beyond survival and expedite our journey home.

Similarly, reading this book may have symbolic value for you, offering hope that you can discover and live your calling. Please don't stop there, however. Open the package. Take out the tools and use them. Everything you need is close at hand. The life God created you to live is within your reach.

Personal Application

(We recommend that when you come to a set of personal application questions in this book, you record your responses in your journal or notebook.)

1. What is your motivation for reading this book? What would you like to see happen in your life as a result of working through it?
2. Reflect on how you would like God to partner with you in this journey of discovering and living your calling. If desired, write a prayer that expresses your thoughts, needs, and hopes.

Live Your Calling

PART ONE

CALLED FOR A PURPOSE

1

IN SEARCH OF A CALLING

*Deep in our hearts, we all want to find and fulfill a purpose bigger than
ourselves. Only such a larger purpose can inspire us to heights we know we
could never reach on our own. For each of us the real purpose is personal and
passionate: to know what we are here to do, and why.* OS GUINNESS

A *USA Today* poll found that if people could ask God just one question, most would want to know, "What's my purpose in life?" Periodically, we find ourselves questioning who we really are and what we
are supposed to do in life. These thoughts may nudge us gently or they
may launch a season of upheaval in our lives.

We may feel unsettled and restless, sensing that there are truths
about ourselves to uncover and mysteries to unravel about why we are
here on earth. We dare to believe that there *is* something special within
us, and that we *do* have a life mission to find and fulfill. We may not be
sure how to discover this purpose but feel driven to do so. Although we
may describe our quest as a search for our calling, we may not be entirely sure what it is that we seek.

Looking for Our Place

"Most of us are looking for a calling, not a job," says Nora Watson in
her interview for Studs Terkel's classic book *Working.* "Most of us . . . have

jobs that are too small for our spirit. Jobs are not big enough for people."
Nora speaks for those who feel trapped in work that provides a paycheck
but gives little room for using their gifts or doing something that is personally meaningful. She compared her job with that of her father, who
had felt his work was "a profession of himself" and a calling.

Throughout our lives we try to find our place in the grand scheme
of things. Marianne, age twenty, voiced the struggle to find her identity
in life: "I believe God is calling me to use my gifts, but I don't know
exactly what they are. I'm trying to figure out what he wants me to do,
but feel rather lost." John, thirty-five, described his need for a new direction: "If I died tomorrow, my years of work will have had little meaningful impact in this world. Success isn't enough anymore. I know I
should be doing something different, but I have no idea what that would
be." At forty-eight, Jackie was taking a new look at herself: "My children are grown and I want to find out what I should be doing now."

A Secular View of Calling

The American culture encourages us to look to our work for our sense
of purpose and calling. Today, "work is fast replacing religion in providing meaning in people's lives. Work has become how we define ourselves. It is now answering the traditional religious questions: Who am
I? How do I find meaning and purpose? Work is no longer just about
economics; it's about identity."[1] We have been told that finding our calling is the same as getting our dream job, doing what we love, or finding
our right livelihood. Therefore we are left feeling "uncalled" if we are
not using our gifts within work we value.

Equating calling with work is not new; it began hundreds of years
ago with the Puritans. In his book *The Call,* Os Guinness describes how
"such words as *work, trade, employment,* and *occupation* came to be used
interchangeably with *calling* and *vocation.* As this happened, the guidelines for callings shifted; instead of being directed by the commands of
God, they were seen as directed by duties and roles in society. Eventually the day came when faith and calling were separated completely."[2]

From this secularized perspective of calling, we are led to believe that we have no more significant purpose than to work.

Without a doubt, work *is* important. Most of us spend 60 percent or more of our lives working. At its best, work uses our unique gifts and abilities and provides opportunities to make a difference in the world around us. Discontentment with work can be agonizing, affecting every area of our lives. Helping you discover your giftedness and find your calling within work and volunteer activities are key goals of this book.

The Bible, however, reveals that work is *not* our central calling. There are no biblical examples of someone being called to paid employment.[3] Although God has designed each of us for special tasks and assignments, his calling for us is much greater and more soul-satisfying than a summons to work.

Called to Know the Caller

Before being called to something, we are called to Someone. Before we are called to *do*, we are called to *be*. Our *primary calling*[4] is to be in a personal relationship with God through faith in Jesus Christ. The Bible tells us that God has *called* us into fellowship with his Son, Jesus Christ.[5] God created us and knows our strengths, weaknesses, dreams, and fears. In spite of our imperfections, God loves us perfectly and completely. He wants us close to him. He calls us to belong to him.

Garrison Keillor recalled painful childhood memories of being chosen last for baseball teams. He dreamed of just one time being picked first—of hearing the team captain say, "'Him, I want *him!*' . . . But I've never been chosen with much enthusiasm."

In contrast, the gospel message is that God chooses each of us with great enthusiasm. None of us is a last pick, or chosen grudgingly. To each of us God says, "You! I want *you!*" God has created us to be his and to have a significant place in this world.

Our primary calling is not tied to our employment. We don't lose our calling if we lose a job. We can live our calling even if we are unemployed or in work that doesn't fit us well. God values us for who we are, not for what we can produce or achieve within work. God's call to us is an eternal one that encompasses and transcends our temporal activities. (See "Your Most Important Calling" on our Website, www.Live YourCalling.com, if you would like to know more about your primary calling to a personal relationship with God.)

When one of us responds to God's call to salvation through faith in Jesus Christ, he or she enters into a new relationship with God[6] and a brand new life.[7] Jesus then calls us to become his disciples, or students, so that we can learn from him how to grow in the knowledge and power of our new life.[8] (See Appendix C for information about the spiritual disciplines and other resources for spiritual growth.) In the New Testament, *calling* represents the life of faith itself. We are exhorted to "walk worthy"[9] of the calling we have received. Dallas Willard describes the crucial idea of discipleship as "learning from Jesus to live *my* life as he would live my life if he were I."[10]

As disciples, we seek to live as God's people wherever we are and in whatever we do. God thus works through our individual lives to do the work of his kingdom. This was beautifully illustrated at a conference on spiritual renewal when a group of participants shared how they had seen God's Spirit at work in their lives in the preceding week.

One woman described how she believed God was using a column she writes in her company's newsletter to bring healing to the dissension-torn organization. Two men brought God's kingdom into a restaurant by praying with their waitress about her fear of developing a debilitating physical condition. A college student taking a class in Eastern religions found that his teacher and classmates were curious about the Christian spiritual disciplines he practiced and were asking him many questions about his faith.

As each person spoke, we were given snapshots of how God was active in the world through the day-to-day lives of his people. God has chosen to do his work on earth through us. He knows who we can become as we follow Jesus. Our primary calling is to travel through life with God, living each day as called people. We live our calling as we walk with God.

Your Individual Calling

Imagine getting a letter from the White House saying the president of the United States needs you for a critical assignment. He has determined that you are the only person in the world who can accomplish the mission. No doubt you would experience a flood of emotions, among them feeling highly valued.

Someone far greater than the president has already sent you this message. The Bible tells us that God has brought you into this world for specific purposes in his eternal plan. You have been born for such a time as this. Ephesians 2:10 tells us that "we are God's workmanship, created in Christ Jesus to do good works, which God prepared in advance for us to do." God has been ahead of us, getting everything ready for our accomplishing what he calls us to do. He is "manipulating all the resources of the universe in order that the work you do may be a part of his whole great and gracious work."[11]

The life of faith opens our eyes to see ourselves and the world around us differently. The closer we walk with God, the more we understand God's agenda for humanity and our part in it. Incredibly, God calls us to be his "fellow workers."[12] Embracing us as his partners to help fulfill his purposes on earth, God calls us to various tasks and life roles. These are our *secondary callings,* which include such life roles as parent, spouse, family member, worker, student, church member, citizen, friend, and neighbor. Our secondary callings provide the contexts in which we can live our primary calling to follow Jesus.

Your work, or *vocational calling,* is one of your secondary callings. It is inextricably connected to your primary calling to be in relationship with God. The English word *vocation* has its origin in the Latin word *vocare,* which means "to call." Your vocational calling is a summons from God to use your gifts in the world, whether it be within paid employment, the home, or volunteer activities.

Guinness explains the crucial distinction between our primary calling and secondary callings: "We can therefore properly say as a matter of secondary calling that we are called to homemaking or to the practice of law or to art history. But these and other things are always the secondary, never the primary calling. They are 'callings' rather than the 'calling.' They are our personal answer to God's address, our response to God's summons. Secondary callings matter, but only because the primary calling matters most."[13]

Johnny Hart's story illustrates how his vocational calling is an expression of his primary calling. Hart is called to be a cartoonist. He has used his long-running comic strips *B.C.* and the *Wizard of Id* to communicate God's truths to people who might never read a Bible or visit a church. At times, the impact has been dramatic. One woman wrote him that a *Wizard of Id* strip saved her from committing suicide. Johnny also finds opportunities to share the hope of Christ with fellow cartoonists and others with whom his work brings him into contact.[14]

The God of Possibilities

Like Johnny Hart, we also have been gifted in specific ways, equipping us for particular vocational callings. When God allows us to glimpse our potential, however, we are often tempted to retreat behind the wall of our perceived limitations ("Gee, God, I'd love to do that . . . but you know, I just can't"). We forget that God has never let human limitations get in the way of his plans for a person. It has been said that God doesn't call the equipped; he equips the called.

God says that his power is made perfect in our weaknesses.[15] He calls us to do things that we cannot do in *our* own power so that we will draw on *his* power. Although he is an award-winning cartoonist, Johnny Hart has only a high school education. He says, "I have always been stupid. I don't have a good memory . . . I've looked up every word in the dictionary almost twenty times." His difficulty with words continuously discouraged him. Even when his career was skyrocketing, he would sit down to read "just a normal book . . . and in one paragraph I'd have to look up five words. And I'd think, man, will I ever have a vocabulary?"[16] Yet God has called him to work that depends on the skillful use of words. God's power shines through our limitations.

God is greater than any obstacle. Each of us has our own personal set of doubts, fears, insecurities, and challenging life circumstances. Some people may feel that they have waited too long and are too old to do what God has called them to do. Lois Prater's story challenges our perceptions about limitations to living our calling at any age.

As a young teen she had promised God she would serve him overseas. But instead she entered into a difficult marriage and never acted on her promise. When her husband died, she once again experienced the desire to serve God in a foreign country. She resisted, however, feeling that at age seventy-six her opportunity had come and gone. "I said, 'Lord, I'm too old to go now. I can't do this,'" Lois admits. But she found she couldn't turn down this second chance to fulfill her childhood promise to God.

So at eighty-seven, Lois Prater has become God's unlikely choice to build an orphanage in the Philippines and rescue thirty-five children from neglect, poverty, and abuse. Lois lives with the orphans in a two-story, two thousand square foot white stucco home. They call her *Lola,* meaning "grandmother" in Tagalog, their native language. Lois says confidently, "I serve a mighty God. He's in control. I feel I'm not talented enough to do any of this. But God enables me. My responsibility is to do what I can."[17]

It's Not Too Late

Many people fear it is too late to do anything of significance with their lives. They may be filled with a profound sense of despair and regret because they feel they have already wasted much of their lives. In our work, clients have made comments such as "I wish I had done career planning twenty years ago. I could have done so much more for the Lord!" or "I really have buried my talents. It's too late to do much now." They find themselves burdened by guilt, remorse, and fear about how God will judge their lives.

Lois Prater's life witnesses to the fact that as long as we are alive it is never too late to live our calling. If we are still alive, we know that we have not yet completed our mission on earth. God can use every-thing in our lives. When we turn to him and seek to live our calling, he can take all of us—our life and work experiences, our successes, our sup-posed failures, our strengths, our weaknesses, our past, our present, and our future—and use it for his purposes and our good.

The Invitation of Grace

Jesus told a parable about workers in a vineyard.[18] In the story, an estate manager hires workers at five times throughout the day. The first come early in the morning; the last are not hired until 5:00 P.M. An hour later the workday is over and it is time for all the men to be paid. Those hired at five o'clock are paid first. Each is given a dollar (in the Message version of this story). When the men who were hired in the early morning see that, they think, "Great! We'll get paid more." When their turn comes, however, they are also paid a dollar. "That's not fair!" they grouse. "Those guys only worked an easy hour while we slaved all day under the hot sun." But the estate manager reminds them that they agreed on the wage of a dollar. "I decided to give to the one who came last the same as you. Can't I do what I want with my own money? Are you going to get stingy be-cause I am generous?"[19]

In this parable Jesus shows us the grace of God. Dallas Willard de-fines *grace* as "the action of God bringing to pass in our lives good things which we neither deserve nor can accomplish on our own."[20] Grace is God's love in action. Willard writes, "God has a plan for each of us in the work he is doing during our lifetime, and no one can prevent this from being fulfilled if we place our hope entirely in him. The part we play in his plans now will extend to the role he has set before us for eternity."[21]

Our gracious God invites each of us to come to work in the vine-yard. It doesn't matter if it is the morning, afternoon, or evening of our lives. Come, you who are weary and heavy-laden. Come, you who feel unworthy. Come, you who have been worshipping other gods. Come, you who have denied me. Come, you who are burned out by all you have been trying to do for the kingdom. Come, learn from me and find rest for your souls.

It doesn't matter what you have been doing up to this moment. God calls you to be a part of his great work in this world, and thereby become the person he created you to be. God is choosing *you* for his team. God has plans for your life; plans that will prosper and not harm you; plans to give you hope and a future.[22] Place your hope entirely in him and respond to his calling to come work with him today. As you grow closer to him and participate more fully in the work he calls you to do, you will find and fulfill the central purpose of your life.

Personal Application

1. Why do you think so many people struggle with the question, "What's my purpose in life?" What is your response to the question?
2. What is your reaction to the idea that your primary calling is to a relationship with God, and that work is one of your secondary callings?
3. In what way can you see yourself being God's "fellow worker"?

2

CALLED TO BE YOU

Before I can tell my life what I want to do with it, I must listen to my life telling me who I am. . . . Vocation does not come from a voice "out there" calling me to become something I am not. It comes from a voice "in here" calling me to be the person I was born to be, to fulfill the original selfhood given me at birth by God.

PARKER PALMER

A central part of answering the question "What is my purpose in life?" is finding your vocational calling. Within you resides a special combination of gifts—talents, interests, skills, personality traits, and much more—that is the foundation of your vocational calling. There has never been anyone else like you in human history, and there never will be another you again. You are called to be "you": the unique, gifted, capable person who was designed by God and created to fulfill a divinely appointed purpose with your life.

Discovering your design and your vocational calling can be challenging, however. We are complex, multilayered beings who develop over time. In addition, the world around us changes rapidly and presents us with a staggering number of choices. How do we know what we should do? How do we know the direction in which God wants us to go?

Our vocational calling emerges out of our relationship with God, so inevitably there is a dimension of mystery to it. God's interactions with us are not wholly understandable, predictable, confinable, or controllable. In trying to discern our vocational calling, therefore, we may feel as though we are in unfamiliar territory. When we are unsure of which way to go, it is helpful to have both a compass and a map.

Compass Principles for Finding Your Vocational Calling

A compass points to true north,[1] which is an objective, external reality that we depend on for direction. Where we *think* true north is or how we *feel* about it does not affect its veracity. Similarly, there are eternal truths that impart a true-north orientation for our lives. We present three biblical "compass principles" here that guide us in the search for our vocational calling.

Life Calling Compass Principle One: God Calls Us to Keep Our Primary Calling Primary

God calls you to be the "you" he created you to be. He knows, however, that you can only become your real self if you give yourself to him. C. S. Lewis wrote, "The more we get what we now call 'ourselves' out of the way and let Him take us over, the more truly ourselves we become. . . . It is when I turn to Christ, when I give myself up to His personality, that I first begin to have a real personality of my own. . . . Sameness is to be found most among the most 'natural' men, not among those who surrender to Christ."[2] Within our relationship with God we can be transformed into the extraordinary individuals he intends us to be.[3]

If we keep our relationship with God at the center of our lives, he also can equip and empower us to do the extraordinary things he designed us to do. The things to which God calls us usually are challenging. In *Experiencing God,* Henry Blackaby says that moving from our way of thinking or acting to God's way of thinking or acting requires us to make major adjustments. We cannot stay where we are and go with God at the same time. We have to be willing to make changes in our lives.

Sometimes the problem in finding our vocational calling is not that we are unclear about God's calling to us, but rather that we are unwilling to do what he is asking. For many of us, financial concerns get in the way of our following where God is leading. Over the years, we have had many people begin their career counseling with us by expressing their desire to do *whatever* God wants them to do with their lives. If their new vocational calling would necessitate living on less income, however, their tendency often was to stay in the same job or field in order to maintain their lifestyle. Living our calling may require confronting some difficult money issues that have no easy solutions.

We also have seen stunning examples of God's faithfulness to people who choose to trust him to meet their financial needs as they pursue their vocational calling. Jim and Jan believed God was calling them to leave their positions in higher education and join Wycliffe Bible Translators, a nonprofit organization. One large obstacle stood in Jan's way, however. She was afraid that if they made this career change, their reduced income would be inadequate to fund a dearly held dream: to send their children (then ages three, eight, and ten) to a Christian college.

In spite of her concern, they made the decision to join the organization and entrust God with their children's education. Nineteen years later, their three children were all graduates of Westmont, a Christian college in Santa Barbara, California. At a time when the national average for undergraduate debt was more than $12,000, all three graduated debt-free. Their story illustrates that God has unlimited resources he can make available to us if we trust him enough to follow where he leads.

Keeping our primary calling primary builds our faith and trust in God so that we are able to answer "Yes!" to his call despite our fears and reservations. We trust that he is calling us toward something that is the very best for us, and we have faith that he will provide what we need to fulfill that calling. Keeping our focus on the Lord also reminds us that our ultimate accountability for what we do with our lives is not to our parents, spouse, boss, neighbors, society, or ourselves. We are called to live our lives playing to an Audience of One: God.

Life Calling Compass Principle Two: God Calls Us to Use Our Gifts to Meet Needs in the World

Your God-given design is a gift from your Creator, and it gives you essential clues about what God wants you to do in the world. Elizabeth O'Connor said, "We ask to know the will of God without guessing that his will is written into our very beings. We perceive that will when we discern our gifts."[4] You may already be aware of some dimensions of your design; other parts may be latent or undeveloped abilities and interests that are yet to be discovered.

God has given us gifts so that we can use them to benefit others, and to bring recognition and honor to him.[5] He does not call us to seek self-fulfillment, but rather to find fulfillment through seeking to serve. Frederick Buechner illuminates what makes work (whether paid or volunteer) a vocational calling:

> Vocation: It comes from the Latin *vocare,* to call, and means the work a [person] is called to by God. There are all different kinds of voices calling you to all different kinds of work, and the problem is to find out which is the voice of God rather than of Society, say, or the Superego, or Self-Interest.
>
> By and large a good rule for finding out is this. The kind of work God usually calls you to is the kind of work (a) that you need most to do and (b) that the world most needs to have done. If you really get a kick out of your work, you've presumably met requirement (a), but if your work is writing TV deodorant commercials, the chances are you've missed requirement (b). On the other hand, if your work is being a doctor in a leper colony, you have probably met requirement (b), but if most of the time you're bored and depressed by it, the chances are you have not only bypassed (a) but probably aren't helping your patients much either.
>
> . . . *The place God calls you to is the place where your deep gladness and the world's deep hunger meet* [emphasis added].[6]

Discovering the skills you love using ("your deep gladness") and the particular needs (the "world's deep hunger") you are enthusiastic about serving directs you toward your vocational calling. *Enthusiasm* comes from the Greek words *en*, meaning "within," and *theos*, "god." We experience enthusiasm when the God-given design inside us connects with needs in the world. Your enthusiasm about meeting particular needs can be an important indicator of the real you, and of your vocational calling.

Modupe discovered how to connect her deep gladness with the world's deep hunger by opening a bookstore in her hometown in Nigeria. Formerly an administrative manager in a bank, she now offers books and resources that encourage self-development. "It was an area that was not being served at all where I live," she says. "I have really enjoyed God's favor in the business. More important, I am doing what I naturally enjoy. Being able to match my customers' needs with particular resources is a very pleasurable part of my work."

Becoming Need-Focused

Our human nature encourages us to focus on our own needs. God, however, calls us to direct our attention to the needs of others. Needs come in all shapes and sizes. Every job meets some type of need.

"Need," as used here, refers not only to fundamental human needs for sufficient food, clean water, safe shelter, adequate health care, and so forth, but also to other things people lack that they desire or find useful, such as a need for a good education or recreational activities. Need can also refer to something required by animals or other living things. Veterinarians, for example, alleviate suffering and meet other needs of pets and livestock.

A key part of finding your vocational calling is discovering which types of needs you enjoy meeting. We experience a greater sense of purpose in our work and volunteer activities when we care deeply about the needs that we are serving.

All Work Can Be Sacred

God cares about all of the needs in this world. He doesn't separate life into sacred and secular categories. The Bible does not support a two-tier view of work, with "full-time Christian service" being in the upper tier and everything else below it.

Christians frequently wrestle with this issue when making career decisions. People who have an intense desire to serve God often think the best place to do so is within a church or Christian organization. On the other side, pastors who feel mismatched with their jobs and are thinking of leaving the professional ministry may feel extremely conflicted as to whether a position outside of the church is a lesser calling.

We can do God's work in the pulpit or in the factory. We are called to be full-time Christians wherever we are and in whatever we do. God calls some of us to work in churches, mission agencies, and Christian organizations. He calls others of us to work in the marketplace.

Andy Stanley emphasizes the importance of our serving in nonreligious contexts: "The truth is that our secular pursuits have more kingdom potential than our religious ones. For it is in the realm of our secular pursuits that secular people are watching. . . . It is there that God desires to demonstrate his power through those who are willing to be used in such a way. . . . [E]very role, relationship, and responsibility carries divine potential."[7]

Life Calling Compass Principle Three: God Calls Us to Proactive Stewardship of Our Gifts

God calls each of us to a life of stewardship. The Bible teaches us that everything we have—our time, skills and abilities, relationships, money and material resources, and the message of the gospel itself—are gifts God entrusts to us to manage and use wisely for the good of his kingdom.

We live in a time and place of tremendous opportunity. With opportunity comes responsibility. Jesus said, "From everyone who has been given much, much will be demanded; and from the one who has been entrusted with much, much more will be asked."[8] We may experience seasons in our lives when we have to take "just a job" to pay the bills and provide for our family. In general, however, we have great freedom in the United States to make choices about what we do to earn a living and where we invest our time. God calls us to use our freedom and opportunities responsibly, exercising stewardship over our time, talent, and treasure.

Jesus' Story About the Stewardship of Our Gifts

Jesus used the "Parable of the Talents" (found in Matthew 25:14–30) to teach us about the stewardship of our gifts. In the story, a master leaves on a long journey, entrusting his money to his three servants. He gives the first servant five talents; the second, two talents; and the third, one talent. The first two servants figure out where they can get the best return on the money and double their investment. The third servant, however, digs a hole in the ground and hides his portion.

When the master finally returns, he settles accounts with his servants. He lavishly praises the first two and rewards them by putting them in charge of many things. The third servant makes excuses for his actions, declaring that he was afraid. He hands the one talent back to the master, saying, "Here is what belongs to you." The displeased master replies that at the very least he could have earned interest on it at the bank. He takes the one talent from the servant's hands, and banishes him from the property.

This parable contains several lessons for us. First, it suggests that *God gives valuable gifts to each of us.* Although the servants were given different amounts of money, each was given a substantial amount. A "talent" was a unit of weight. In today's dollars, one talent of gold would be worth more than $500,000! The parallel metaphorical meaning of "talents" in the parable is a reference to our God-given gifts. Given that the monetary examples are large amounts, we can deduce that even a "one talent" person is given a significant measure of ability.

Second, *we only are responsible for what we have been given.* The servant given two talents was not held accountable for producing as much as the one given five talents. On that day that each of us stands before God, we will not be compared with anyone else. The measuring stick will not be Billy Graham or Mother Teresa, or any of the spiritual giants who have lived in the centuries before us.

What we do with our lives will be judged only in light of what we could have done with the specific gifts that God chose to give us. We only have to be who God has created us to be; we are called to accomplish only what he has designed us to do.

Third, *we need to be proactive and take risks* in order to invest and multiply our gifts. The servants were not told what to do with their talents. They had to plan and make decisions about how to invest them. They also had to risk in order to achieve results that would please their master. Fear stopped the third servant from investing his talents. Fear is a normal human emotion, but it is not an acceptable excuse for inaction. We need to learn how to manage our fear so that it doesn't prevent us from being good stewards of our gifts and living our calling.

Assessing Vocational Fit

One means of evaluating how well you are doing as a steward of your gifts is assessing the level of vocational fit, or degree of match, between your God-given design and your work. ("Work" refers to your primary occupation, whether it is within paid employment, the home, or volunteer activities.) We discuss five levels of vocational fit here. As you read, see which level best describes where you are at this point in your life.

The lowest level of vocational fit is when a person sees his or her work as *just a job*. A level one job may provide a paycheck but little sense of enjoyment or satisfaction. Sometimes we need to get just a job to pay the bills, but most people typically want to move on as quickly as possible. Level two is *OK work* that is of some interest. Many people get stuck at this level. Although they may feel somewhat discontented, there may not be enough dissatisfaction to motivate them to make a change—particularly if they are making a good salary.

At level three of vocational fit, people find themselves in *enjoyable work* that may be satisfying for many years. Once people have achieved competency in their work, however, they may experience a need for something more meaningful. Level four is *meaningful work*, in which people feel they are contributing to a significant purpose or giving something back. People at this level usually are in work that is a good fit for their skills, but sometimes they are most motivated by the mission of the organization. As a secretary in a large Christian organization commented, "While I enjoy my work, what's most significant for me is that even when I'm filing, I feel like I'm contributing to the cause of world evangelism."

Level five of vocational fit is *vocational integration*. At the highest level of vocational fit, a person's work is an expression of who he or she is. Some well-known people whose lives exemplify vocational integration are Mister Rogers (an innovator in children's television programs); Zig Ziglar (motivational speaker); Elizabeth Dole (senator, public servant); Charles Schultz (creator of "Peanuts"); Truett Cathy (founder of Chick-fil-A restaurants); Mary Kay Ash (CEO, Mary Kay Cosmetics); and Orel Hershiser, Michael Chang, and David Robinson (athletes).

People who have achieved vocational integration in the work world seem to earn their living by being themselves. Their unique design is clearly visible in what they do; their personal identity is merged with their work identity. They feel that they are doing the type of work they were meant to do. Passionate about their work, level five individuals make life choices that allow them to pursue additional opportunities and professional growth.

Doing God's Work

Any job, regardless of how well it fits, gives us an opportunity to live our primary calling by being God's representative in the workplace. In any job, we are called daily to exhibit a gracious attitude of service toward our boss, coworkers, customers, and others. We are called to avoid gossiping, complaining, speaking unkindly about people, lying, and cheating by not working diligently and to the best of our ability. There may even be times that God uses us to share the gospel and meet another's spiritual needs. In our job, as in every aspect of our lives, we are called to be God's people.

When we think about being good stewards of our gifts and finding our vocational calling, however, we do need to consider our potential within the levels of vocational fit. Moving up the levels requires effort, discipline, persistence, risk, and often sacrifice. The compass principle of being a proactive steward of our gifts directs us to consider where we are within the levels and where we need to be.

The higher we move up, the more opportunity we typically have to do *God's work* within the context of *our work*. The more we use our giftedness, the more influence we usually have in work situations and life in general. When others see a person's giftedness in action, and the person is recognized for excellence in his or her work—whether it be in running a company or managing a home—there is increased respect for and willingness to listen to that person. More opportunities present themselves. Our sphere of influence grows.

Proverbs 22:29 says, "Do you see a man who excels in his work? He will stand before kings; he will not stand before unknown men." The greater our reputation for excellence in what we do, the more we gain attention and can use our influence for God's purposes.

The enormous amount of media attention given to Mel Gibson's film *The Passion of the Christ* was due largely to his stature as an actor and director in the film industry. In the weeks surrounding its release, major magazines, newspapers, and television networks ran numerous stories related to the film. We watched in amazement as Roger Ebert, the film critic, explained the message of the gospel during his film review on national TV. Jesus came to earth to die for our sins, said Ebert. "That was his mission." People who might never before have thought about the meaning of Christ's death now found themselves confronted with it everywhere. Gibson's movie made Jesus' life and death a hot topic of conversation in a culture that is usually reticent to speak his name except as a profanity.

One doesn't have to be famous, however, to make an impact. Karole Shirley worked for a national temporary services agency. The welfare recipients who wanted to work touched her heart. Investing countless hours with each client, she taught them the skills they would need to make it in the business world. She lent them money from her own pocket and even invited some of them to her church. Not only did her clients succeed but her office's net profits also rose by 300 percent in one year as people flooded her office.

The success of Shirley's office stood out to the company's CEO and eventually came to the attention of President Bill Clinton in a discussion of welfare reform. Her company began opening new offices around the country that focused on recruiting inner-city residents. She was promoted and given a new role of helping to market the new offices and develop strategic alliances with local businesses.[9] Her work became a means for using her gifts and expressing her highest values. Shirley's level of commitment and excellence created the opportunity to influence decision makers for the good of others.

Vocational Calling as a Lifelong Journey

In the movie *City Slickers*, Mitch (played by Billy Crystal) tries to find his way through a midlife crisis and discover the meaning of life by going on a cattle roundup. Curly (Jack Palance), the gruff trail boss, tells Mitch that the secret of life is just one thing. When Mitch asks him to reveal what that one thing is, Curly tells him he'll have to figure that out for himself.

People have expressed to us their desire to find that one thing they are called to do. As we talk with them, we sometimes find that they are making particular assumptions about their vocational calling. Their operational belief is that there *is* one thing (usually meaning a specific job or career path) out there somewhere (at a particular company) for them to find. Once they have found that one thing out there somewhere, they believe they will then be set for life and not have to deal anymore with troublesome questions about what to do with their lives. We find that a need for security and fear of change typically underlie these beliefs.

The problem with this perspective is that it does not fit with either the biblical record or the real world of work in the twenty-first century.

God's people have usually found themselves doing a series of things in their lives. For example, the New Testament shows us that even though Paul's job title of "apostle" didn't change, he found himself doing things and going places he could not have imagined or anticipated on his own. This seems to be a rather typical pattern when God is actively involved in a person's life.

In addition, change is the hallmark of today's workplace. Few people will work for the same company their entire lives. Mergers, closures, and organizational retooling in response to the competition and rapid-fire change in our world today ensure that most people will hold several jobs during their working years, either by choice or necessity. Even people who have reached vocational integration and are paid for being themselves have to reorient and reposition themselves at various points in their lives.

Living your vocational calling is a journey. As you grow and mature, God can use you in new and more significant ways. Your journey may take you through the levels of vocational fit one step at a time, such as progressing from just a job to OK work to enjoyable work. As you continue on your journey, investing the time and energy needed and being willing to risk, you can move up the levels of vocational fit.

When you are progressing in using your gifts to make a contribution in this world—even if you have only moved thus far from just a job to OK work—you are living your vocational calling. Although it is possible to do so, most people don't move from just a job to vocational integration in just one job change. Most of us experience a series of transitions in our lives, but each step is an important part of the process of living our calling. Our vocational calling is an ongoing journey, not a destination. Your vocational calling therefore is not about finding and doing one thing; rather, it is doing many things for God, the Audience of One.

Duane's story illustrates how a vocational calling unfolds over the years. He was working at a car rental agency when he came to us for career counseling. Although he had received several promotions and was excelling in his work, he felt what he was doing lacked sufficient meaning.

His purpose in doing career planning was to figure out where he should be investing his abilities to be the best possible steward of his gifts. A natural visionary, he loved using his creativity, marketing, and networking skills to grow an organization and make a difference in people's lives. God has increasingly used him over the years because Duane and his wife, Tricia, have been willing to take risks, persevere, grow, and be obedient to what they believed God was calling them to do.

His work has included directing a nonprofit organization that taught entrepreneurship to low-income young people, founding a nationwide youth entrepreneurship company, writing a values-based curriculum about Christian youth entrepreneurship, cofounding and directing the northern California chapter of an organization that helped senior business executives make a difference in the lives of others, and helping organizations grow and fulfill their missions more effectively.

We asked him what God has taught him thus far in his life about his vocational calling. Duane responded, "He is teaching me to continue to be purposeful in how I employ my 'design,' and *not* to be afraid to leave an area where I am not using the gifts and skills he has given me, but rather to pursue leveraging those gifts, skills, talents, and passions for his kingdom! I have learned that when I do take a step of faith and go in the direction where I think I can best be used, God meets me there and multiplies my 'loaves and fishes' in ways I could never imagine."

On the journey of living your vocational calling, you will discover the truth in this equation: You + God's power = Enough. You are enough because God has designed you perfectly to fulfill your intended purpose.[10] You are enough because God will work through you with his limitless power.[11] You are enough because he loves you and can transform you.[12] You are called to be you, and he who calls you is at work within you. You can be empowered to be yourself today; you can become the you God has always intended you to be. The truth is that "God can do anything— far more than you could ever imagine or guess or request in your wildest dreams!"[13]

Personal Application

1. Life calling compass principle one is "God calls us to keep our primary calling primary." On a scale of 1 to 5 (1 = little sense of connection with God; 5 = consistent focus on God), how well are you doing with this principle? What would you like to do differently to deepen your relationship with God?
2. With which servant in the Parable of the Talents (Matthew 25:14–30) do you most identify?
3. How does thinking of yourself as the *manager* rather than the *owner* of your gifts affect how you make life choices?
4. Five levels of vocational fit (just a job, an OK job, enjoyable work, meaningful work, vocational integration) are described. Which level best describes your current or most recent job? Why?

PART TWO

CREATING YOUR
LIFE CALLING MAP

3

MAPPING YOUR DESIGN

We're all pilgrims on the same journey—but some pilgrims have a better map.

NELSON DEMILLE

Experienced explorers traveling in new territory use both a compass and a map. The compass principles—keeping your primary calling primary, using your gifts to meet needs, and being a proactive steward of your gifts—direct you in your journey of finding God's purposes for your life. In this chapter you will create your own map to use in the search for your vocational calling.

A map enables you to determine where you are, the location and distance of your destination, and the best route for getting there. It helps you to anticipate what you might encounter on the trip. An accurate map also gives you a sense of confidence when making decisions during the journey. For the journey of living your calling, you need a detailed map of your God-given design that identifies the gifts you have to invest in the world. Your map helps you position yourself for maximum impact with your life.

Creating Your "Mental Map"

Cartography is the art and science of map making. Each of us is the cartographer of a "mental map" of how we see our design and ourselves. Your mental map includes your beliefs about what you can and can't do, what interests you and what doesn't, what is and isn't important to you, and what your personality is or isn't like.

Your mental map might lack sufficient detail to be helpful or even contain erroneous information that can hinder you in discovering your vocational calling. The outcome of your search for your vocational calling depends greatly on the accuracy of your mental map.

"I like helping people" was the centerpiece of Sandra's mental map of her design. She had bounced from one job to another over the years, trying to find her place in the world of work. She came to realize that she needed a more specific map of her design, since almost any job would allow her to help others in one way or another.

Determining the kinds of people she most wanted to help, the settings that would fit her best, and most important, how she wanted to help people, enabled Sandra to create a much more useful map for herself. The more precise and customized your map, the more beneficial it will be to you in your journey.

Many of us also have mental maps with at least some degree of inaccuracy. Tom believed he was a poor public speaker. His interest in becoming a sales trainer, however, required that he confront his long-held belief. During a counseling session, he recognized that his negative image of his speaking ability was based on one traumatic incident that happened in high school, more than fifteen years earlier.

Tom discovered that with additional training and experience he not only had the potential of being a very good speaker but also enjoyed it. By correcting his mental map so that it more accurately reflected his skills and interests, he was able to recognize and pursue work roles that fit his design.

Life Experiences Shape Our Mental Maps

Our life experiences shape and color our mental maps. During our growing-up years we are exposed to a variety of skills and interest areas through our family, school experiences, recreational activities, work settings, friends, books, and the media. From our own personal collection of experiences, we tend to develop beliefs about what we can and can't do, and things that interest us and things that don't.

Direct experience is important in creating our mental maps. We may, however, make inaccurate determinations about our skills, abilities, and interests because of limited exposure, negative experiences, inadequate training, or our own fears and insecurities. The problem with depending solely on our life experiences to create a map of our gifts, abilities, and interests is that it may be incomplete, as it is entirely dependent upon the opportunities and situations we have encountered.

Voices That Alter Our Maps

Feedback from others about our ability and potential is another powerful force that shapes our mental map. For better or for worse, parents have a tremendous influence on their children's self-image. Many adults view themselves in the light of their parents' negative comments from years before: "You'll never make money doing that. Why don't you do something practical?" or "You'll never be good enough to succeed at that. When are you going to grow up and let go of your silly dreams?"

Most of us have a vocal "committee" assembled in our heads, made up of influential people from our past and present. Committee members can be our parents, family members, teachers, pastors and other significant adults, peers in school, bosses, coworkers, and others who have given us messages about ourselves and our potential over the years.

The messages we hear from supportive committee members can encourage us to press ahead, assuring us that there are great possibilities for our lives. Often, however, there are also some voices whispering things that discourage us and cause us to doubt that we will ever find and fulfill our purpose in life. Our mental maps may therefore reflect the opinions of our committee, but not the reality of who we are.

Making Your Map Accurate

Developing a thorough understanding of your design requires using a variety of assessment tools. Your design is too complex to be assessed by only one test, inventory, or exercise, which is why you complete a variety of self-assessment exercises in this book. The assessments help you develop increased awareness of how the dimensions of your design fit together. You also gain a deeper understanding of how your intrinsic God-given design can be used in the world.

A good assessment process lays the foundation for determining which types of careers or volunteer options most likely fit you best. No assessment, however, can tell you which specific job you should do. Over the years, we have had many people say something like, "I took that test in high school and it told me I should be a bus driver." Or a farmer. Or a teacher. Comments of that sort reflect either a misunderstanding of the assessment or poor interpretation on the part of the person explaining the results. No good career assessment narrows the field to just one job title, or even a few.

Many people would like to find the magic test that tells them which type of work fits them best. No such test exists, however. The world of work is much too large and human beings are too complex for this to be possible. Thousands of different types of jobs exist already, and new jobs are created continually. No test can possibly catalogue every job nor assess all of the relevant factors for matching an individual with a job.

Used appropriately, however, good assessments *do* help illuminate the important parts of your design and expedite the process of identifying the types of jobs or volunteer options that fit you best. Assessments can assist you in developing an accurate mental map of your God-given design. They can help you fill in formerly blank areas, clear up confusing or conflicting information, and bring previously unclear areas into focus.

Creating Your Life Calling Map

Your Life Calling Map and a completed sample Life Calling Map are found at the end of this chapter on the pages with the shaded borders. The map has four parts: Mission Statements, Dimensions of My Design, Priority Goals, and Action Plan. In this chapter, you will complete the second part of the map, Dimensions of My Design. After finishing the assessment exercises in this chapter (transferable skills, core work values, preferred roles, personality type, compelling interests, and spiritual gifts), you will enter your results in your map, creating a vital record of key dimensions of your God-given design.

The Dimensions of My Design is the heart of your map. You will be using it in a variety of ways to help you discover exciting career and volunteer options and discern which direction to go in your life. You will complete the other three parts of your map (Mission Statements, Priority Goals, and Action Plan), adding to the usefulness of your map, in Chapter 10.

Your completed map will serve as a tangible record of your understanding of your God-given design and be a foundation for discovering your calling. Your map is a helpful tool to use as you go through this book. Here are how others have benefited from their Life Calling Maps:

> My Life Calling Map has shown me how I can use my skills, interests, values, and abilities in a way that will serve God best. Without this help I would have wasted many years going in the wrong direction, never trying or knowing what God had put in my heart to do.

> It helped me understand the ways God has gifted me (vocationally, spiritually, personally) and what he is calling me to do with my gifts.

> Over the years, I've come back to my map many times. It has enabled me to make midcourse corrections and decisions about job changes with confidence.

> My Life Calling Map has helped me understand and accept my God-given mission in life. It's given me an opportunity to earnestly

assess myself, learn who I am, acknowledge my capabilities, and feel free to move without fear into a more rewarding future.

As you complete the self-assessment exercises in this chapter, you will be drawing from, reorganizing, adding to, and perhaps challenging your current mental map of how you see your design. Developing an accurate map of your design helps you see the real you—the person God created you to be—and to manage your gifts and abilities intelligently.

ASSESSMENT ONE: TRANSFERABLE SKILLS

Transferable skills are abilities that can transfer, or be taken, from one setting and be used in another. For example, Jill took the teaching and organizing skills she had developed as an elementary school teacher into the business world to her new job as a corporate trainer. John took the cooking skills he had honed at home and put them to use preparing meals once a week in a shelter for the homeless. Transferable skills can be gained on the job as well as in your hobbies, leisure pursuits, responsibilities at home, and volunteer activities.

With this inventory, you identify skills you have developed and select the skills you particularly enjoy using. You also identify skills you would like to develop; these may be skills you will want to use in a significant way in the future.

Transferable Skills Inventory

Directions, Part One

1. Read through the entire list of skills and place a check in the *C* column next to each skill in which you are *competent*. (Competent means that you have at least average ability in the skill.) You might have developed competency in the skills in any context; you do not need to have used them in a paid work setting.
2. Read through the list of skills again, this time placing a check in the *E* column next to each skill that you *enjoy* using (or *think* you would enjoy using, if you currently have little or no experience using the skill).
3. Review the skills you have marked as ones you enjoy using. Circle the names of the skills that you *most* enjoy using (or *think* you would enjoy using) in a work or volunteer ministry/service context. (We recommend choosing about eight to fifteen skills.)

After you have completed these steps, go on to Part Two of the directions, located after the list of transferable skills.

C	E	
		1.
		Assemble/Construct: Build machines, furniture, buildings, etc., using mechanical, construction, or carpentry skills
		Drive/Fly: Maneuver a car, truck, plane, etc. (could include high-speed or emergency situations)
		Enforce compliance: Request, demand, or force people to obey rules, laws, policies, etc.
		Handle emergency situations: Take appropriate action in situations related to fires, crime, accidents, etc.
		Install: Place machinery, devices, etc., in position for service or use
		Landscape: Develop a plan for modifying an outdoor area using trees, plants, grass, etc.
		Move with agility: Partial or whole-body movement using coordination, strength, or endurance

C	E	1. continued
		Operate equipment: Use manual dexterity or physical movement to run tools, office machines, or other machinery
		Patrol: Watch over and guard areas or people to maintain orderliness and safety
		Provide physical, manual, or skilled labor: Perform services such as painting, cleaning, laying flooring, etc.
		Repair/Service: Fix mechanical things; restore machinery to functional operation
		Transport: Move materials, objects, or people from one location to another in a vehicle or by physical strength
		Work with animals: Raise, tend, train, or treat domestic or wild animals
		Work with plants: Perform activities related to planting and maintaining flowers, trees, fruits and vegetables, lawns, and other plants
		2.
		Analyze/Evaluate: Appraise, critique, assess, examine, study, judge
		Categorize/Classify: Sort, arrange, order, or label concepts, things, etc.
		Check for quality: Inspect objects or places for compliance with specific standards
		Estimate: Determine the approximate value or cost of something or the amount of materials required for a project
		Perform tests: Check and measure the performance, quantity, or quality of equipment, machines, food, substance, processes, programs, people, etc.
		Solve problems/Troubleshoot: Generate and implement solutions to resolve difficulties
		Research/Compile data: Systematic discovery using investigation, observation, experiments, interviews, or written resources
		Use math formulas: Use statistical or mathematical formulas to make calculations with data
		Write computer programs: Develop computer programs to store, locate, and retrieve specific information; use computer languages
		3.
		Compose music: Write original music or variations of musical compositions

continued on the next page

C	E	3. *continued*
		Cook/Prepare food: Prepare, cook, bake, or arrange food or meals with regard for nutrition and visual appeal
		Design/Create: Artistically plan or form a work of art, decorative scheme, program, etc.
		Edit: Revise or rewrite written materials to improve content or style
		Entertain/Perform: Act, sing, dance, play a musical instrument, speak, announce, etc., for an audience
		Illustrate/Portray images: Sketch, draw, paint, photograph, videotape
		Improve/Modify: Change or adapt in order to enhance, refine, make better
		Make artistic handicrafts: Create decorative or useful items that are visually appealing
		Synthesize: Integrate diverse parts into a new whole
		Translate/Interpret: Explain ideas and concepts so that they are more easily understood (usually involves foreign language or sign language)
		Write: Express ideas, facts, and information in articles, books, advertisements, etc.; may be creative, informative, or technical material
		4.
		Advise/Counsel: Give information, suggestions, and recommendations; urge adopting a course of action
		Diagnose: Determine causes of physical, emotional, or spiritual problems
		Encourage/Motivate: Inspire, stimulate, and strengthen others; instill courage, spirit, or confidence
		Host/Offer hospitality: Welcome people to a place or event; make them feel comfortable; attend to their needs
		Listen: Pay thoughtful, careful attention to both information and feelings expressed by a person
		Mentor/Coach: Instruct, advise, support a person to assist his or her personal or professional development
		Prescribe treatment: Recommend course of action to help physical, emotional, or spiritual problems
		Provide medical care: Administer first aid, treat, nurse, rehabilitate, heal, cure, etc.
		Provide personal services: Guide people to locations; serve food or beverages; take care of skin, hair, nails, etc.

C	E	
		4. *continued*
		Refer to resources: Direct people to useful information, places, people, etc.
		Teach/Train/Speak: Present, explain, clarify, or summarize information; speak before or facilitate groups
		5.
		Influence/Persuade: Stimulate others to take action or change an opinion or belief
		Manage money: Strategize for use of money; prepare budgets, plan investments, etc.
		Mediate/Act as a liaison: Serve as intermediary between two or more parties (may be for purpose of resolving conflict)
		Negotiate: Deal or bargain to gain settlement or agreement
		Plan: Devise a strategy for accomplishing an objective
		Purchase/Buy: Obtain goods and services through exchange of money or other payment
		Represent: Take the place of a person, group, or organization; speak and make arrangements on behalf of the other party
		Sell/Promote: Convince someone of the value of a product, service, idea, or concept
		Supervise/Manage: Oversee carrying out work assignments by others
		6.
		Attend to details: Pay attention to small items, parts, or elements with carefulness and thoroughness
		Calculate/Compute: Determine by mathematical methods or reasoning
		Coordinate/Make arrangements: Schedule, coordinate, handle logistical details for people or events
		Manage records: Collect, classify, or record information; update records as needed
		Organize: Categorize, systematize details, papers, physical things, work flow, etc.
		Type/Enter data on a computer: Use manual dexterity to input data using a keyboard
		Verify accuracy: Check written materials, financial records, or other data for errors
		Work with financial data: Prepare, audit, balance financial information, etc.

Directions, Part Two

1. Notice the blank numbered row above each of the six sets of skills. In each numbered row, write in the "skill cluster category" name and its abbreviation. In the first blank row, for example, write *Physical (P)*. (The skill cluster category names were omitted from the inventory so that you would not be influenced by them as you completed the assessment.)

   1. Physical (P)
   2. Analytical (AN)
   3. Creative (CR)
   4. Helping (H)
   5. Managing/Persuading (M/P)
   6. Detail/Organizing (D/O)

2. Review the skills you have circled. Then, in the transferable skills section of your Life Calling Map: Dimensions of My Design (which is located at the end of this chapter), write the following *in prioritized order* (most enjoyed, second most enjoyed, and so forth).

   The skills you would most enjoy using in a *work* setting

   The skills you would most enjoy using in a *volunteer ministry/service* setting

   The skills you would like to explore or develop further

(An example is provided in the completed sample Life Calling Map, located just before the Life Calling Map on which you will record your results.)

3. Observe which skill cluster categories (physical, analytical, and so on) in the transferable skills inventory contain the most circled skills. In the skill cluster categories section of your Life Calling Map, record

   The two or three skill cluster categories that best represent the skills you would enjoy using in a *work* setting

   The two or three skill cluster categories that best represent the skills you would enjoy using in a *volunteer ministry/service* setting

The skill clusters categories table on the next page gives information about typical career and volunteer interests for each of the skill cluster categories.

SKILL CLUSTER CATEGORIES

Skill Cluster	Characteristic Career and Volunteer Ministry/Service Interests*
Physical (P)	Activities that involve working with plants (including food-producing plants, flowers, trees, shrubs, lawns, etc.) or animals (breeding, tending, training, etc.) *Sample career areas:* landscaping, gardening, horticulture, botany, farming, forestry, zoology, veterinary medicine, animal training *Sample volunteer activities:* helping with church's landscaping; camp settings that include activities in nature or with animals; activities that include farming, ranching, or animal husbandry; training animals for service activities
	Activities that involve precise, ordered use of objects, tools, and machines *Sample career areas:* skilled trades such as electronics, carpentry, equipment operation, and construction *Sample volunteer activities:* maintaining and repairing buildings and machines of church or nonprofit organization; new construction or remodeling; driving a van or bus; teaching hands-on skills to others in a ministry/service context; running audiovisual equipment at church
	Activities that may involve some element of physical risk *Sample career areas:* law enforcement, security, emergency response, sports *Sample volunteer activities:* directing traffic and crowd control at large events; sports and outdoor activities at a camp; providing emergency medical care in disaster settings
Analytical (AN)	Activities that Involve exploring and examining physical, scientific, and cultural things to understand and control them *Sample career areas:* science, engineering, inspection, research, technical, and computer-related *Sample volunteer activities:* writing computer programs; setting up or maintaining Websites of church or nonprofit organization; tutoring youth in science, math, computers; helping others understand relationship between science and Christianity
Creative (CR)	Activities that involve use of physical, verbal, or human material to create art forms or products *Sample career areas:* music, art, writing, and drama *Sample volunteer activities:* using drama or music in worship or evangelism; writing press releases, articles, curriculum for church or nonprofit organization; using arts and crafts as outreach event; conducting camp to develop artistic abilities of youth

continued on the next page

SKILL CLUSTER CATEGORIES, *continued*

Skill Cluster	Characteristic Career and Volunteer Ministry/Service Interests*
Helping (H)	Activities that involve interaction with other people for their enjoyment or to inform, train, develop, cure, educate, or otherwise assist them *Sample careers:* education, ministry, social welfare, counseling, customer service *Sample volunteer activities:* teaching classes at church or a nonprofit organization; hosting a neighborhood Bible study; serving in a lay counseling ministry; participating in medical ministry; facilitating small group or social activities
Managing/ Persuading (M/P)	Activities that involve persuading or influencing others, typically within a business context *Sample career areas:* sales, management, leadership, legal, political, and self-employment *Sample volunteer activities:* developing publicity materials for church or nonprofit organization; raising funds for church or nonprofit; leading a church board or committee
Detail/ Organizing (D/O)	Activities that involve precise, ordered use of data: keeping records, calculating, managing an office, organizing numerical and written data, and working with finances *Sample career areas:* financial, computer-related, and clerical *Sample volunteer activities:* taking minutes for boards and committees; organizing church activities and events; helping others organize their homes or finances; keeping financial records for church or nonprofit organization.

Note: * See Chapter Five for additional information and strategies for linking skill clusters to specific jobs.

Understanding Your Results

Most people find they have some clear patterns emerge after completing the transferable skills inventory and reviewing the skill cluster categories. Here is some additional information to help you analyze your results so you can more fully understand the meaning and usefulness of the patterns.

Your Most Enjoyed Skills. On your Life Calling Map you listed the skills you would most enjoy using within work and volunteer activities. Using skills that energize you greatly increases your sense of satisfaction and enjoyment within your career and volunteer pursuits.

You may have listed some transferable skills in which you have little or no ability currently but that you believe you would enjoy using at some future time. These are skills that potentially can be used in a longer-range career transition (once you have had a chance to become competent in them) or that can be tried out and developed in a hobby, leisure pursuit, or ministry setting. Church and other volunteer settings are great places to try out and develop new skills.

Your Most Marketable Skills. A marketable skill is one that you can perform competently and that is attractive to a potential employer. Obviously, your job target will dictate which of your skills are most marketable. If you are seeking a position as an accountant, the fact that you are a great cook is of little relevance. However, if you want to be a pastry chef, your ability to *cook or prepare food* is of prime importance.

In looking for a new job or career, seek to identify and then target the type of work that uses your most enjoyed skills. Your most enjoyed skills will then be also your most marketable ones. If you love to design and create, for example, then you will be happiest in work that heavily uses those skills (such as interior decorating, desktop publishing and graphic design, landscape architecture).

If, however, you find yourself between jobs or facing an imminent layoff and need to find work quickly, focus your job search on positions similar to those you have had before that use your most developed work skills. Making a career transition into a new career area that uses different skills usually takes longer than finding something similar to what you did before or are doing. (For example, an unhappy accountant who needs to find work quickly should probably target finance-related jobs that use skills similar to those used in a previous or current job.) Once you find a new job that pays the bills, you can begin taking steps toward a transition into a career that uses skills you enjoy.

Your "Killer Skills." Your "killer skills" are those in which you are competent—for which perhaps you are even renowned—but that you really dislike using. Whenever you have to use them, you can feel the energy draining out of you. They certainly can kill you emotionally or, taken to the extreme, create so much stress that you suffer physical symptoms and disease.

For example, Beth was a labor relations attorney who did well in her job. She received lots of positive feedback from her clients and other attorneys. Every day, however, she dreaded going to work and being in situations that involved rancorous, high-stakes bargaining. Persuading and negotiating were killer skills for her. In the same way, house painters who dislike painting, teachers who don't enjoy teaching, and salespeople who would rather do almost anything other than sell are all examples of people in jobs that require spending a majority of their time using killer skills.

Do you have any killer skills? (Review the transferable skills inventory and note skills that you marked you are competent in but dislike using.) If so, do they cluster in a particular category? Does that category relate to your present work? If it does, and if you are using your killer skills much of the time, you most likely have already experienced some negative effects. You may only be seeing comparatively minor stress-related symptoms such as headaches, stomach distress, or irritability right now, but if you don't do something to reduce the amount of time you spend using your killer skills your symptoms are likely to get worse.

Can you avoid using killer skills altogether? Probably not, but a suggested target to aim for is using your killer skills no more than 20 percent of the time in a given day or week. Make it a goal to get into a job (or volunteer activity) that minimizes use of your killer skills and maximizes your using skills you most enjoy. You and those around you will reap the benefits.

Frequently Asked Questions About Transferable Skills

You may have some questions about the results from your transferable skills inventory. Here are some of the questions that frequently arise.

- *What if my top skills are from more than three categories?* The most common pattern is for your most-enjoyed skills to occur primarily in two or three categories. If you find your skills are distributed among four or more categories, review the skill cluster category descriptions to see if you can choose the two or three categories of most interest to you in your career or volunteer activities.

If you find that you still can't decide on three categories or fewer, it may indicate that you will benefit from learning more about career options or ministry/service options. (We address ways of doing this in Part Three of this book.) You may need more exposure to the world of work to be able to identify the categories that best fit your interests. (This is common for young people, who have not been in the work force for an extended time, as well as those who have been in one type of work for several years.)

Another possibility is that the category or categories associated with your top one, two, or three skills are the most important to you and should be used to guide you in your career exploration. For example, Jane had *sell/promote* and *influence/persuade* as her top two skills, but they were the only two representing the managing/persuading skill cluster category. The remaining skills on her Life Calling Map were divided among three other categories. These two skills, however, were ones that Jane knew she loved to use. She should consider focusing on careers or ministry/service activities within the managing/persuading skill cluster category. She doesn't need to be concerned that at this point there are no other skill cluster categories of high interest to her.

- *What if I have few skills I feel I am competent in using?* This can be an age-related issue; the younger a person is, the less time or opportunity he or she has had to develop a range of skills. More common reasons for checking off too few skills as ones you are competent in, however, relate to perfectionism, being too hard on oneself, and struggling with low self-esteem. We encourage you to ask two or three friends (or other people who have observed you doing a variety of things) to give you feedback on which skills they think you perform competently. We suggest having at least two people evaluate your skills so you can observe the commonalities and differences in their assessments.

• *What if I have few skills checked as ones I enjoy using?* This can be characteristic of someone whose job has been a poor fit for a long time, or who has had limited opportunities to try out a range of skills. Perhaps you have not tried many skills in your life and simply have not experienced many skills you really enjoy using. You may benefit from experimenting with some other skills. Choose some you *think* you would really enjoy, and find a low-risk way to try them out. Or use skills you currently have in another setting. A burned-out kindergarten teacher, for example, might find she loves teaching adults. (Remember, you may need to try a skill several times to find out if you really enjoy it. Few people, for example, enjoy giving their first public speech. It may take time to get over the fear and become a good enough speaker to enjoy it.)

We have also observed that some people are conservative in how they experience or describe their emotions. They very rarely, if ever, describe something as "really good" or "great." "It was fine" might be a more typical response when asked to describe something they liked. People of this type often tend to answer in the negative if they are unsure about how they feel. Therefore, if they are unsure about whether or not they enjoy particular skills, they are likely to leave the space blank instead of placing a check in the *E* column of the inventory to indicate they enjoy using the skill. If you have a similar tendency, we suggest you go back over the list and check off any skills you enjoy even a little. You don't have to be wildly enthusiastic about something in order to place a check in the *E* column.

Also, if you are experiencing some degree of depression you may not feel very excited about or interested in much of anything. If such feelings persist, consider seeking professional assistance from a pastor, counselor, or other qualified person.

• *What if I have checked most or all of the skills as ones I can perform competently?* The longer a person lives, the more skills he or she typically has the opportunity to develop. Similarly, the more types of work a person has done (paid or unpaid), generally the more skills he or she develops. Still, it would be rare for a person to be equally competent in most or all of the skills in this assessment. You may want to reevaluate your competency in the skills and apply a higher standard of performance. (You may also want to solicit some help from your friends or work associates in evaluating your competency level in these skills.) A discriminating assessment of your skills makes it easier for you to determine which of your skills really are most enjoyable and most marketable.

Personal Application

1. How can identifying your most-enjoyed transferable skills help you in discerning your vocational calling?
2. Are there any killer skills you find yourself having to use too much in your work or life right now? If so, what are they? What changes could you make to reduce the amount of time you use them?

ASSESSMENT TWO: CORE WORK VALUES

Values are beliefs about what is important in our lives. *Core values* are ones that are deeply rooted and have compelled us to pursue certain life choices and avoid others. Many forces shape our core values, among them other people (especially our family of origin), our life experiences, education, and spiritual beliefs.

At various points in our life we may encounter a need to take a time out to reassess our values. During our teens and twenties, we typically examine and question values passed on to us by our family. We begin to assess which values we will adopt as our own and which we want to discard, a process that can continue into midlife and beyond. The forties are commonly a time in which we reevaluate our lives and the values we have used thus far to chart our course. The values of the surrounding culture we once may have embraced, such as placing great importance on material possessions and financial wealth, may be seen in a new and less positive light. As we age, recognition of our mortality and the brevity of life increasingly shape our values.

Assessing Your Core Work Values

People often have a hard time making decisions when they are unclear about what really is important to them. The clearer you are about which values are important to you—and why—the easier it is to make important decisions in your life. Many of your values are also relevant in making choices about volunteer opportunities in your church and community. The better a volunteer position fits you, the more motivated you will be in the role.

Your assessment results are most meaningful and helpful if they are based on an honest self-appraisal. You might be tempted to choose values you think are the best or right ones to have—resulting in a profile of some fictitious person. Telling yourself the truth about your core values deepens your understanding of your motivations, desires, past decisions, current struggles, and best choices for your future.

Core Work Values Inventory

Directions

1. From the inventory given here, choose the values that are personally important to you (even if your current job or volunteer activity emphasizes different ones). For each value, rate how important it is to you according to this scale:

    1 *Not important at all* to me in my work or volunteer ministry/service activities

    2 *Somewhat important* to me in my work or volunteer ministry/service activities

    3 *Important* to me in my work or volunteer ministry/service activities

    4 *Very important* to me in my work or volunteer ministry/service activities

2. Circle the five work values that are most important to you at this point in your life.

3. Record your five circled values *in prioritized order* in the Core Work Values section of your Life Calling Map.

_____ *Achievement/Excellence:* Attain a high level of proficiency in my work

_____ *Affiliation:* Be recognized as a member of a particular group or organization

_____ *Autonomy:* Can determine the nature of my work and the use of my time without significant interference from others

_____ *Balance:* Have sufficient time in my personal life for the people and activities that are important to me

_____ *Challenge:* Opportunity to take on difficult or complex tasks

_____ *Change/Variety:* Have work responsibilities or other opportunities that frequently vary in content and setting

_____ *Competition:* Engage in activities that pit my abilities against others, with clear win-or-lose outcomes

_____ *Control:* Be in charge of people or factors that have an impact on my life and work

_____ *Creativity/Innovation:* Create new ideas, programs, organization, structures, or anything else, not following a format previously developed by others

_____ *Decision making:* Opportunity to make key decisions

_____ *Excitement/Adventure:* Experience frequent or a high degree of excitement or adventure in the course of my work

_____ *Expert status:* Be regarded as a person of high intellectual prowess or as one who is an acknowledged expert in a given field

_____ *Financial gain:* Do work in which I have the likelihood of earning a large amount of money

_____ *Friendship:* Opportunity to work with others I like; develop close personal relationships with others at work that extend beyond the workplace

_____ *Help others:* Be involved in helping other people directly or indirectly; do something that makes a positive contribution to others in this world

_____ *Influence people:* Be in a position to change attitudes or opinions of other people

_____ *Knowledge:* Engage myself in the pursuit of knowledge, truth, and understanding

_____ *Power/Authority:* Control the work activities (and to some degree, destinies) of others

_____ *Prestige:* Be seen by others as having power, wealth, success, or importance

_____ *Professional advancement:* Have the opportunity to gain increasing stature or higher-level positions in my work

_____ *Recognition:* Be recognized for the quality of my work in some visible or public way

_____ *Security:* Feel "safe" in my job and organization

_____ *Self-expression:* Experience receptiveness from others to my vital ideas, feelings, or perspective

_____ *Stability:* Have a work routine and responsibilities that are largely predictable and not likely to change over a long period of time

_____ *Teamwork:* Connect with others in working toward a common goal

_____ *Time flexibility:* Have freedom to determine my own schedule for being at work and completing tasks

_____ *Work alone:* Opportunity to work on projects by myself the majority of the time

Personal Application

1. Why is each of your top values important to you?
2. How have your values had an impact on your life choices (positive or negative)?

ASSESSMENT THREE: PREFERRED ROLES

A "role" can be defined as the part a person plays in a given event, circumstance, or time period. Your roles, and how you carry them out, flow out of your unique combination of skills and abilities. Although you can perform a variety of roles (in paid or volunteer positions), some feel more natural and are more enjoyable than others. These are your "preferred roles." This inventory helps you identify one or more preferred roles that you enjoy taking on in work or volunteer activities.

Preferred Roles Inventory

Directions

After reading through the descriptions of the roles, complete these activities.

1. Identify one, two, or three preferred roles you would most like to take on within work:

   _____

   _____

   _____

2. Identify as many as three preferred roles you would most like to take on for volunteer ministry/service positions within your church or community:

   _____

   _____

   _____

3. Identify any role(s) you would like to explore or develop further:

   _____

   _____

   _____

4. Transfer your answers to the Preferred Roles section of your Life Calling Map.

Preferred Roles	Sample Types of Transferable Skills Used	Description
Roles emphasizing CREATING		
Designer/Creator	Design/create; synthesize; improve/modify; write; compose music; landscape; write computer programs; illustrate/portray images; assemble/construct; cook/prepare food	May enjoy coming up with new ways of looking at problems and situations in order to find innovative solutions or strategies; may be a "big-picture" person who is able to create a workable plan to bring a vision into reality. May enjoy creating something new, such as written work, music composition, program, curriculum, play, arrangement of physical space, etc.
Performer	Perform/entertain	Enjoys using skills in speaking, singing, dancing, playing music instruments, etc., in front of an audience.

continued on the next page

Preferred Roles	Sample Types of Transferable Skills Used	Description
Roles emphasizing LEADING/CONTRIBUTING		
Coordinator	Mediate/act as liaison; coordinate/ make arrangements	Enjoys serving as a key person connecting people and resources for accomplishing a goal.
Contributor/ Investor	Manage money; purchase/buy	Enjoys giving money or material goods to support specific people or enterprises.
Leader	Plan; design/create; influence/persuade; supervise/manage; encourage/motivate	Enjoys creating a vision or direction for a group or organization. May oversee other managers to coordinate work activities and goal attainment.
Manager	Supervise/manage; influence/persuade; encourage/motivate	Enjoys working under a respected leader, helping to coordinate the activities of one or more groups, departments, etc., toward accomplishing set goals.
Team or Group Leader	Supervise/manage; teach/train/speak	Enjoys working closely with a small group of people, managing their activities toward accomplishing set goals and creating a cohesive, well-functioning team or group. May enjoy facilitating discussions in a learning or problem-solving environment such as a class or small group setting.
Roles emphasizing PERSUADING		
Negotiator	Influence/persuade; negotiate, listen	Enjoys helping two or more individuals or groups reach an agreement or solution.
Promoter	Sell/promote; influence/persuade	Enjoys talking enthusiastically and persuasively about the merits of someone or something to others.
Recruiter	Sell/promote; influence/persuade; encourage/motivate	Enjoys influencing people to become involved in a cause, project, event, organization, etc.
Seller	Sell/promote; influence/persuade	Enjoys convincing people to purchase or invest money in someone or something.

Preferred Roles	Sample Types of Transferable Skills Used	Description
Roles emphasizing HELPING/INSTRUCTING		
Counselor	Listen; advise/counsel	Enjoys helping people better understand their personal problems, develop solutions, and take action to improve their life situation.
Mentor/Coach	Advise/counsel; listen; motivate/ encourage; teach/train/speak; move with agility	Enjoys interacting in a one-on-one relationship, helping person develop his or her gifts and abilities to achieve a new level of personal or professional growth.
Reconciler	Listen; mediate/ act as liaison; advise/counsel	Enjoys bringing harmony and healing to relationships between individuals or dissenting parties in an organization; skilled in bringing about relational restoration.
Teacher/Trainer/ Speaker	Teach/train/speak; facilitate; perform/entertain; encourage/motivate	Enjoys helping others learn; able to communicate clearly. May teach concepts, factual information, or skill development. May also have an interest in inspiring others.
Roles emphasizing HELPING/ASSISTING		
Caretaker (people)	Provide personal service; listen; provide medical care; manage records; drive/transport; coordinate/make arrangements	Enjoys providing personal care to individuals needing assistance, such as children, the elderly, the ill, or disabled. May involve assisting with physical needs, with the home, finances, etc.
Caretaker (things)	Install; repair/service; analyze/evaluate; check for quality; operate equipment; provide physical, manual, or skilled labor	Enjoys being in charge of specific things or a specific place or area. Oversees upkeep and maintenance; performs or arranges for repair, servicing, etc.

continued on the next page

Preferred Roles	Sample Types of Transferable Skills Used	Description
Roles emphasizing HELPING/ASSISTING, *continued*		
Host/Hostess	Host/provide hospitality; coordinate/make arrangements	Enjoys making people feel welcomed and comfortable within a specific environment. Creates an atmosphere of warmth; sensitive and attentive to people's needs. Help ensure people have a pleasant experience.
Organizer	Organize; categorize/classify; coordinate/make arrangements; attend to details	Enjoys making something orderly and efficient. May enjoy organizing things, information, people, or multiple details, as for an event.
Recordkeeper	Manage records; attend to details; calculate/compute; verify accuracy; work with financial data; type/enter data on a computer	Enjoys entering data, maintaining records, and keeping track of information regarding people, money, events, or other things.
Supporter/Helper	Could use a variety of skills depending on the need	Enjoys helping others where needed. May prefer a behind-the-scenes role. Likes pitching in to help with the task at hand. Enjoys being of service to others.
Roles emphasizing ANALYZING/SOLVING PROBLEMS		
Evaluator	Analyze/evaluate; check for quality; estimate	Enjoys assessing the quality of someone or something.
Troubleshooter	Analyze/evaluate; solve problems/ troubleshoot	Enjoys solving problems. Able to assess a problem situation quickly and determine appropriate action. May involve crisis or risk taking.

Preferred Roles	Sample Types of Transferable Skills Used	Description
Other role(s)		
Specialist (on your Life Calling Map, name your particular specialty)	(The skills used depend on the type of specialty)	Ability to perform specific and specialized skills involving information, people, or things. Can do something that requires special training and experience. May involve using technical or mechanical skills or other hands-on skills such as carpentry, construction, landscaping, painting, etc.
Other Role:	_____	_____
	_____	_____
	_____	_____
	_____	_____

Personal Application

1. Describe opportunities you have had to take on each of your top three roles.
2. What relationship do you see between your most-enjoyed transferable skills and your most-preferred roles?

ASSESSMENT FOUR: PERSONALITY TYPE

One important dimension of your design is your personality type, or temperament type. God has built certain preferences into your design; your unique combination of preferences makes up your personality. John, for example, prefers working directly with other people most of the time; by contrast, Jennifer likes having extended periods of time to work alone. Anita prefers completing one project before beginning another, while having several projects going on at one time energizes Chris. Their preferences greatly influence the type of work and volunteer ministry/service activities and environments they find appealing.

Understanding your preferences, or personality type, helps you identify work and volunteer situations that fit *your* design. Although you can work outside of your preferences, doing so for long is stressful. You are most motivated and energized when you can be yourself. Typically, you are being the best steward of your gifts and abilities when you are working out of—and not against—your personality type.

Over the years we have reviewed many personality and temperament assessments. The personality inventory we have found to be by far most helpful to our clients is the Myers-Briggs Type Indicator® (MBTI) instrument,[1] which assesses key preferences on four distinct dichotomies or scales:

How you are energized	Extraversion (E) vs. Introversion (I)
How you acquire information	Sensing (S) vs. Intuition (N)
How you make decisions	Thinking (T) vs. Feeling (F)
How you deal with the outside world	Judging (J) vs. Perceiving (P)

Determining which preference on each of the four scales best describes you (such as E or I, S or N) results in a four-letter code for your personality type. Each of the sixteen combinations, or personality types, has its own strengths and weaknesses. Understanding your natural strengths can help you determine the places in which you can best contribute.

Isabel Briggs Myers (one of the developers of the MBTI® instrument) quotes from Romans 12:4–6 (KJV) in the beginning of her book, *Gifts Differing:* "For as we have many members in one body, and all members have not the same office: So we, being many, are one body . . . and every one members one of another. Having then gifts differing. . . ." The Church and the world need each of the personality types.

Understanding the strengths, weaknesses, and gifts of your personality type can help you discover and recognize areas to which God may be calling you. The better you understand your preferences, the better you can discern the types of positions in which you will find enjoyment and have the potential to make a significant contribution.

Personality Type Inventory

Directions, Part One

1. Review the two lists of contrasting preferences and check off any phrases that describe your *typical* preferences.
2. Decide which of the two preference scales or categories (for example, Extravert or Introvert) is *more* descriptive of you. (Most people have some preferences in each category but find one category is more

descriptive of them. Select the preference category that *better* describes you.)

Extravert (E)	Introvert (I)
☐ Energized by active involvement in events; like to be immersed in a breadth of activities.	☐ Energized and excited when involved with the ideas, images, memories, and reactions that are a part of their inner world.
☐ Most excited when around other people; may also have an energizing effect on those around them.	☐ Often prefer solitary activities or spending time with one or two others with whom they have an affinity.
☐ May be seen as go-getters or people persons.	☐ May be seen as calm and centered or reserved.
☐ Like to solve problems by talking aloud and hearing what others have to say. May act too quickly.	☐ Like to solve problems by thinking about the issue before talking with others or taking action. May not act quickly enough.
☐ May enjoy being involved in many activities.	☐ May like focusing on one activity in depth and dislike interruptions.
☐ Tend to have many acquaintances and friends.	☐ Prefer fewer, more intense relationships.
☐ Are often drawn to activities with high people contact, out-of-office activities, and variety.	☐ Are often drawn to activities requiring solo projects or one-on-one contact, continuity, and concentration.
☐ Enjoy learning through activity and discussion.	☐ Enjoy learning through reflection and mental rehearsal.

Overall, which preference scale best describes you? Extravert (E) or Introvert (I) ____

Sensing (S)	Intuition (N)
☐ Often seen as realistic and practical, and good at grasping the facts and details.	☐ Often seen as imaginative and insightful, and good at grasping the big picture.
☐ Focus more on the present than the future.	☐ Focus more on the future than the present.
☐ Often patient and careful with precise work and routine, and like the chance to hone a skill.	☐ Often patient in projects with many intangibles and possibilities, and enjoy new ways of doing things.

continued on the next page

Sensing (S)	Intuition (N)
☐ May solve problems by working through things systematically to gain understanding; work from the facts to the big picture.	☐ May solve problems through quick insight and through making leaps; work from the big picture to the facts.
☐ Like having established procedures for doing something; uncomfortable when directions or expectations are unclear.	☐ May be interested in doing things that are new and different; may prefer minimal structure to allow room for creativity.
☐ May tend to prefer working at a steady pace.	☐ May prefer a rhythm of working intensely for a period of time followed by down time.
☐ Put experience first, and place less trust in words and symbols.	☐ Place great trust in insights, symbols, and metaphors and less in what is literally experienced.
☐ May focus so much on the facts of the present or past that they miss new possibilities.	☐ May focus so much on new possibilities that they miss the practicalities of bringing them into reality.

Overall, which preference scale best describes you? Sensing (S) or Intuition (N) ____

Thinking (T)	Feeling (F)
☐ Prefer to understand experience through logical thinking.	☐ Prefer to understand experience in the context of human relationships.
☐ Seek objective truth and fairness, regardless of effects, and may be seen as forthright and firm.	☐ Seek harmony and cooperation, sometimes ignoring the consequences, and may be seen as warm and understanding.
☐ Naturally critique to detect errors or inconsistencies.	☐ Naturally appreciate the merits of others.
☐ Concerned with determining the objective truth in a situation, logical consistency, and analysis of cause and effect.	☐ Concerned with personal values and with making decisions on the basis of what is the best for the people involved in a situation.
☐ Value finding the truth in a situation, even if it is a truth or principle that is independent of what they or others might want to believe or wish were true.	☐ Value relatedness between people; often concerned with establishing or maintaining harmony in their relationships.
☐ Make decisions with their heads and want to be fair.	☐ Make decisions with their hearts and want to be compassionate.

continued on the next page

Thinking (T)	Feeling (F)
☐ Believe telling the whole truth is more important than being tactful.	☐ Believe being tactful is more important than telling the cold truth.
☐ May miss seeing or valuing the "people part" of situations and be experienced by others as too task-oriented, uncaring, or indifferent.	☐ May miss seeing or communicating about the hard truth of situations and be experienced by others as too idealistic, mushy, or indirect.

Overall, which preference scale best describes you? Thinking (T) or Feeling (F) ＿＿

Judging (J)	Perceiving (P)
☐ Value order, structure, and pre-dictability, and like completing tasks.	☐ Value spontaneity and the challenge of dealing with the unexpected.
☐ Want matters decided and settled, and take deadlines and schedules seriously.	☐ Like to leave options open and may let other interesting developments interfere with deadlines.
☐ May appear task-oriented; like to make lists of things to do.	☐ May prefer keeping laid-out plans to a minimum.
☐ Like to get their work done before playing.	☐ Like to approach work as play or mix work and play.
☐ Plan work to avoid rushing just before deadline.	☐ May work in bursts of energy, and enjoy rushing just before deadlines.
☐ May dislike having to interrupt working on one project and switch to a different one.	☐ May begin many projects but have trouble finishing them.
☐ May make decisions too quickly without sufficient information.	☐ May stay open to new information so long that they miss making decisions.
☐ May focus so much on the goal or plan that they miss the need to change direction at times.	☐ May focus so much on adapting to the moment that they do not settle on a direction or plan.

Overall, which preference scale best describes you? Judging (J) or Perceiving (P) ＿＿

Directions, Part Two

1. Write the four letters you have chosen: ____ ____ ____ ____
   (example: E S F P). If you just cannot decide between one or more
   of the pairs, for now write both letters (example: E/I S F P).
2. Read through the description of your four-letter type in the following pages, highlighting any phrases that particularly describe you.
3. Write your four-letter personality type and key descriptive phrases
   from the personality type inventory and from the type descriptions
   on your Life Calling Map.

Descriptions of the Sixteen Personality Types

Here are descriptions of the typical characteristics and work preferences
for the sixteen personality types. These profiles describe some of the most
common preferences for each personality type; you may find that you have
all of the preferences described for your four-letter type or only some of
them. The characteristics given for each type are *descriptive* rather than *pre-
scriptive*. That is, they describe how the sixteen types typically function;
they do not prescribe how each type will function in every situation. We
can function outside of our preferences, as when an introvert acts as
though he or she is an extravert when hosting a party. However, if we have
to operate outside of our preferences too often or for too long, we may
experience stress and a sense of not being ourselves.

ISTJ

For ISTJs (introvert, sensing, thinking, judging) the dominant quality in
their lives is an abiding sense of responsibility for doing what needs to
be done in the here-and-now. Their realism, organizing abilities, and command of the facts lead to their completing tasks thoroughly and with great
attention to detail. Logical pragmatists at heart, ISTJs make decisions on
the basis of their experience and with an eye to efficiency in all things.
ISTJs are intensely committed to people and to the organizations of which

they are a part; they take their work seriously and believe others should do so as well.

ISTJs are most likely to find interesting and satisfying those careers that make use of their depth of concentration, their reliance on facts, their use of logic and analysis, and their ability to organize. ISTJs are very often found in management careers, particularly in the areas of government, public service, and private business, and they are often found in technical and production-oriented careers as well. Their task orientation, realistic grounding, dependability, and respect for the facts often draw them to careers that call for an organized approach to data, people, or things. These same qualities can also lead to effectiveness as managers.

Examples of careers often chosen by ISTJs are management in business or government, accounting, engineering, computer operations and analysis, technical or trade, teaching, police and corrections work, and skilled trade and crafts work.

ISFJ

For ISFJs (introvert, sensing, feeling, judging) the dominant quality in their lives is an abiding respect and sense of personal responsibility for doing what needs to be done in the here-and-now. Actions that are of practical help to others are of particular importance to ISFJs. Their realism, organizing abilities, and command of the facts lead to their thorough attention in completing tasks. ISFJs bring an aura of quiet warmth, caring, and dependability to all that they do; they take their work seriously and believe others should do so as well.

ISFJs are most likely to find interesting and satisfying those careers that make use of their depth of concentration, their reliance on facts, their warmth and empathy, and their ability to organize. ISFJs are often found in careers that involve nurturing or healing others and also in some spiritually-oriented careers. Their sense of duty, personal commitment, and practicality often draw them to careers in which they can support and be of service to others. These same qualities can also lead to their effectiveness in helping and health-oriented careers.

Examples of careers often chosen by ISFJs are teaching (particularly K-12), medical fields with high patient contact (including family medicine and nursing), religious work, library careers, office and clerical work, and social service work.

ISTP

For ISTPs (introvert, sensing, thinking, perceiving) the driving force in their lives is to understand how things and phenomena in the real world work so they can make the best and most effective use of them. They are logical and realistic people, and are natural troubleshooters. When not actively solving a problem, ISTPs are quiet and analytical observers of their environment, and look for the underlying sense in any facts they have gathered. ISTPs often pursue variety and even excitement in their hands-on experiences. Although they do have a spontaneous and even playful side, what people often first encounter with them is their detached pragmatism.

ISTPs are most likely to find interesting and satisfying those careers that make use of their depth of concentration, their reliance on facts, their use of logic and analysis, and their adaptability. ISTPs are found in a variety of careers but are most drawn to careers that require a tough-minded analytical and realistic approach. Their quiet adaptability, realistic grounding, and willingness to critically analyze the facts often draw them to careers where they can take a pragmatic approach to problem solving. They may also manifest a great curiosity about things, not so much in an abstract search for meaning but a curiosity about how and why they work and about their application.

Examples of careers often chosen by ISTPs are military or corrections work, farming, skilled trade and crafts work, mechanics, electrical and electronic engineering or technical work, computer programming, law, and accounting.

ISFP

For ISFPs (introvert, sensing, feeling, perceiving) the dominant quality in their lives is a deep-felt caring for living things, combined with a quietly playful and sometimes adventurous approach to life and all its experiences. ISFPs typically show their caring in practical ways, since they often prefer action to words. Their warmth and concern are generally not expressed openly, and what people often first encounter with ISFPs is their quiet adaptability, realism, and "free spirit" spontaneity.

ISFPs are most likely to find interesting and satisfying those careers that make use of their depth of concentration, reliance on facts, warmth and empathy, and adaptability. ISFPs are very often found in careers that allow direct practical care of people or hands-on detail work that may require much solitude. Their realistic grounding, depth of feeling, and highly personal approach to life often draw them to careers where they can help others in pragmatic ways. Though often hidden, their warm and sympathetic nature can be felt by others who know them, and they communicate kindness in ways that make them exceptional candidates for working with people in need, children, or animals. Their idealism and deep feeling make them particularly sensitive to the suffering of others.

Examples of careers often chosen by ISFPs are health care and service work, nursing, office or clerical work, personal service careers, skilled craft, trade, and technical careers (such as carpenter, surveyor, radiology technician), police or detective work, and teaching (particularly K-12).

INTJ

For INTJs (introvert, intuition, thinking, judging) the dominant force in their lives is their attention to the inner world of possibilities, symbols, abstractions, images, and thoughts. Insight in conjunction with logical analysis is the essence of their approach to the world; they think systemically. Ideas are the substance of life for INTJs; they have a driving need to understand, to know, and to demonstrate competence in their areas of interest. INTJs inherently trust their insights, and with their task orientation they work intensely to make their vision into reality.

INTJs are most likely to find interesting and satisfying those careers that make use of their depth of concentration, their grasp of possibilities, their use of logic and analysis, and their ability to organize. INTJs are very often found in academic, scientific, theoretical, and technical positions that require prolonged periods of solitary concentration and tough-minded analysis. Their task orientation, powers of abstraction, perseverance, and willingness to look at situations or systems in creative ways often draw them to careers where they can pursue implementation of their inner vision. Their trust in their own insights, faith that they see into the true meaning behind events, and willingness to bring their insights into practical real-world application often communicate to others an impression of confidence and competence, even drivenness. Though these qualities often lead to their being placed in executive and management positions, INTJs are intensely individualistic and resist being bound to routine.

Examples of careers often chosen by INTJs are law, engineering, architecture, physical and life sciences, psychology and social science, computer science, writing and editing, careers in the arts, and consulting.

INFJ

For INFJs (introvert, intuition, feeling, judging) the dominant quality in their lives is their attention to the inner world of possibilities, ideas, and symbols. Knowing by way of insight is paramount for them, and they often manifest a deep concern for people and relationships as well. INFJs often have deep interests in creative expression as well as issues of spirituality and human development. Although their energy and attention are naturally drawn to the inner world of ideas and insights, what people first encounter with INFJs is likely to be their drive for closure and for application of their ideas to people's concerns.

INFJs are most likely to find interesting and satisfying those careers that make use of their depth of concentration, grasp of possibilities, warmth and empathy, and ability to organize. INFJs are often found in careers where creativity and facilitating human development are primary activities. Their orientation to people, confidence in their insights into the nature of things and people, and fertile imagination often attract them to careers where they can draw out the possibilities in others. These same qualities can also lead to exceptional empathic abilities.

Examples of careers often chosen by INFJs are the ministry, education (including religion, foreign languages, and the arts), architecture, medicine, psychology, media and marketing work, counseling, and fine arts.

INTP

For INTPs (introvert, intuition, thinking, perceiving) the driving force in their lives is to understand whatever phenomenon is the focus of their attention. They want to make sense of the world—as a concept—and they often enjoy opportunities to be creative. INTPs are logical, analytical, and detached in their approach to the world; they naturally question and critique ideas and events as they strive for understanding. INTPs usually have little need to control the outer world, or to bring order to it, and they often appear quite flexible and adaptable in their lifestyle.

INTPs are most likely to find interesting and satisfying those careers that make use of their depth of concentration, their grasp of possibilities, their use of logic and analysis, and their adaptability. INTPs are very often found in academic, theoretical, and technical positions, many of which require prolonged periods of solitary concentration and tough-minded analysis. Their concern with ideas and their natural curiosity about the underlying principles and explanations for events often draw them to careers where an in-depth understanding of some abstract subject is required. Their abilities to become absorbed in an idea, to concentrate to the exclusion of all distractions, and to be objectively critical and creative often lead to their gaining a remarkable understanding of some complex problem, issue, or subject matter.

Examples of careers often chosen by INTPs are physical and life sciences, computer science, social sciences, architecture, law, careers in the arts and entertainment, photography, writing and journalism, engineering, and medicine.

INFP

For INFPs (introvert, intuition, feeling, perceiving) the dominant quality in their lives is a deep-felt caring and idealism about people. They experience this intense caring most often in their relationships with others, but they may also experience it around ideas, projects, or any involvement they see as important. INFPs are often skilled communicators, and they are naturally drawn to ideas that embody a concern for human potential. INFPs live in the inner world of values and ideals, but what people often first encounter with them in the outer world is their adaptability and concern for possibilities.

INFPs are most likely to find interesting and satisfying those careers that make use of their depth of concentration, grasp of possibilities, warmth and empathy, and adaptability. INFPs are often found in careers where there are opportunities for caring and communicating, or where there are opportunities to help others. Their highly personal approach to life, sensitivity to people, and willingness to look beyond what is present and obvious often draw them to careers in which they can foster growth and development in others. They also may possess an ability to establish rapport with others quickly, and excellent communication skills.

Examples of careers often chosen by INFPs are fine arts careers, writing and journalism, psychology and psychiatry, social sciences, counseling, architecture, education (religion, art, drama, music, and foreign languages), library careers, acting, and entertainment.

ESTJ

For ESTJs (extravert, sensing, thinking, judging) the driving force in their lives is their need to analyze and bring into logical order the outer world of events, people, and things. ESTJs like to organize anything that comes into their domain, and they will work energetically to complete tasks so they can quickly move from one to the next. Sensing orients their thinking to current facts and realities and thus gives their thinking a pragmatic quality. ESTJs take responsibility seriously and believe others should do so as well.

ESTJs are most likely to find interesting and satisfying those careers that make use of their breadth of interests, reliance on facts, use of logic and analysis, and ability to organize. ESTJs are often found in careers that require the use of tough-minded, fact-oriented, and goal-directed analysis to provide leadership and direction, and they are often found in high numbers in management and administrative positions. They are usually comfortable applying their standards of what is correct, efficient, and sensible to all aspects of their environment. They can therefore be highly analytical and matter-of-fact in their evaluation not only of situations but of people as well.

Examples of careers often chosen by ESTJs are management careers (in retail, business, restaurant, banking, public service, and government), teaching in technical fields or the skilled trades, careers in the military, police and corrections work, social or public services, accounting, and construction.

ESFJ

For ESFJs (extravert, sensing, feeling, judging) the dominant quality in their lives is an active and intense caring about people and a strong desire to bring harmony into their relationships. ESFJs bring an aura of warmth to all that they do, and they naturally move into action to help others, organize the world around them, and get things done. Sensing orients their feeling to current facts and realities and thus gives their feeling a hands-on pragmatic quality. ESFJs take their work seriously and believe others should do so as well.

ESFJs are most likely to find interesting and satisfying those careers that make use of their breadth of interests, reliance on facts, warmth and empathy, and ability to organize. Their energy, warmth, and compassion suit them to work in any field in which they have direct contact with others, and they are often skilled in promoting and supporting fellowship and harmony. Their tendency to idealize whatever they find valuable, along with their high regard for tradition and community, can lead to great loyalty to their organization or the people with whom they work.

Examples of careers often chosen by ESFJs are teaching (particularly K-12 and adult education), religious work (all forms of ministry and education), health care (including nursing and health education), personal service work, child care, household and domestic services, and office and clerical work.

ESTP

For ESTPs (extravert, sensing, thinking, perceiving) the dominant quality in their lives is their enthusiastic attention to the outer world of hands-on and real-life experiences. ESTPs are excited by continuous involvement in new activities and pursuit of new challenges. They tend to be logical and analytical in their approach to life, and they have an acute sense of how objects, events, and people in the world work. ESTPs are typically energetic and adaptable realists who prefer to experience and accept life rather than to judge or organize it.

ESTPs are most likely to find interesting and satisfying those careers that make use of their breadth of interests, reliance on facts, use of logic and analysis, and adaptability. ESTPs are found in a variety of careers but are most often drawn to careers that require an active, realistic, and hands-on approach. Their friendliness, flexibility, and tolerance of the realities of a situation can make them quite skillful in handling interpersonal conflict. These qualities, in conjunction with their use of a more objective and analytic approach to decision making, can make them superbly pragmatic problem solvers and skilled in convincing or negotiating with others.

Examples of careers often chosen by ESTPs include marketing and sales, police or corrections work, skilled trades and craft work, construction work, banking, farming, management in small businesses and government, and journalism.

ESFP

For ESFPs (extravert, sensing, feeling, perceiving) the dominant quality in their lives is enthusiastic attention to the outer world of hands-on and real-life experiences. ESFPs are excited by continuous involvement in new activities and new relationships. They also have a deep concern for people, and they show their caring in warm and pragmatic gestures of helping. ESFPs are typically energetic and adaptable realists, who prefer to experience and accept life rather than judge or organize it.

ESFPs are most likely to find interesting and satisfying those careers that make use of their breadth of interests, reliance on facts, warmth and empathy, and adaptability. They are inclined to put more trust in, and learn well from, firsthand experience, and they have an active curiosity about the world in which they live. ESFPs thoroughly enjoy being with others; active curiosity leads them to seek ongoing involvement not only with people but also in all things physical.

Examples of careers often chosen by ESFPs are teaching (particularly preschool through grade 12) and coaching, child care work, clerical and office work, recreational work, food service, nursing, sales, personal services, and religious work and education.

ENTJ

For ENTJs (extravert, intuition, thinking, judging) the driving force in their lives is their need to analyze and bring into logical order the outer world of events, people, and things. ENTJs are natural leaders who build conceptual models that serve as plans for strategic action. Intuition orients their thinking to the future and gives their thinking an abstract quality. ENTJs actively pursue, and direct others in pursuit of, goals they have set, and they prefer a world that is structured and organized.

ENTJs are most likely to find interesting and satisfying those careers that make use of their breadth of interests, grasp of possibilities, use of logic and analysis, and ability to organize. ENTJs are often found in careers that require drive, leadership, innovation, and tough-minded analysis. They are often quite aware of power and status issues. They are usually comfortable applying a clear sense of what is correct, efficient, and effective to all aspects of their environment. They can therefore be analytical and matter-of-fact in their evaluations not only of situations but of people as well. Their approach to other people tends to be impersonal, and they value competence in others, even as they value it in themselves.

Examples of careers often chosen by ENTJs are a variety of management and administrative positions, business and finance, marketing, psychology and social sciences, law, physical and life sciences, teaching (particularly at the university level), consulting, human resources, and computer sciences.

ENFJ

For ENFJs (extravert, intuition, feeling, judging) the dominant quality in their lives is an active and intense caring about people and a strong desire to bring harmony into relationships. ENFJs are openly expressive and empathic people who bring an aura of warmth to all that they do. Intuition orients their feeling to the new and to the possible; thus they often enjoy working to manifest a humanitarian vision, or helping others develop their potential. ENFJs naturally and conscientiously move into action to care for others, organize the world around them, and get things done.

ENFJs are most likely to find interesting and satisfying those careers that make use of a breadth of interests, grasp of possibilities, warmth and empathy, and ability to organize. ENFJs are often found in careers that require organization, expressiveness, and an interest in people's emotional, intellectual, and spiritual development. Their orientation to people, desire for harmony, and imagination often attract them to these careers, and these same qualities often lead to developing excellent skills in understanding and working with others. Their willingness to see the viewpoints of others, tolerance of diverse opinions, and enthusiasm often gives them exceptional skills in working with groups.

Examples of careers often chosen by ENFJs are religious professions (in all areas of ministry, including religious education), teaching, counseling and psychology, acting, music, fine arts, writing and journalism, library work, and health care professions (including family practice medicine, nursing, and health education).

ENTP

For ENTPs (extravert, intuition, thinking, perceiving) the dominant quality in their lives is their attention to the outer world of possibilities; they are excited by continuous involvement in anything new, whether it be ideas, people, or activities. They look for patterns and meaning in the world, and often have a deep need to analyze and understand the nature of things. ENTPs are typically energetic, enthusiastic people who lead spontaneous and adaptable lives.

ENTPs are most likely to find interesting and satisfying those careers that make use of their breadth of interests, grasp of possibilities, use of logic and analysis, and adaptability. ENTPs are found in a variety of careers that reflect a diversity of interests, but the fields in which they work typically allow them to engage their inventive and analytical minds. Their creativity, comfort with the abstract, and problem-solving abilities often attract them to careers in the fields of science, communications, and technology. They are almost driven to start new projects or envision new ways of doing things, and because they are so stimulated by complexity and new problems to solve they are often found in careers where troubleshooting plays a part. In addition, whatever career they choose must give them a stream of new challenges. ENTPs are not inclined to sit still for long.

Examples of careers often chosen by ENTPs are photography, marketing, public relations, journalism and writing, engineering, computer sciences, life and physical sciences, construction, consulting, acting, arts and entertainment, and law.

ENFP

For ENFPs (extravert, intuition, feeling, perceiving) the dominant quality in their lives is their attention to the outer world of possibilities; they are excited by continuous involvement in anything new, whether it be ideas, people, or activities. Though ENFPs thrive on what is possible and what is new, they also experience a deep concern for people as well. They are especially interested in possibilities for people. ENFPs are typically energetic, enthusiastic people who lead spontaneous and adaptable lives.

ENFPs are most likely to find interesting and satisfying those careers that make use of their breadth of interests, grasp of possibilities, warmth and empathy, and adaptability. ENFPs are often found in careers that are characterized by interests and abilities in working with people and fostering their growth, or that require skills in communication and expression, whether in oral or written form. Their interest in symbols, meaning, and human relationships often attracts them to careers where they can be active, involved with others, and pursue new horizons. Their imagination and enthusiasm lead them to be innovative in whatever they have chosen as a career, and they are almost driven to think of new projects and new ways of doing things.

Examples of careers often chosen by ENFPs are counseling, teaching (particularly at the high school and university level), psychology, journalism and writing, social science, fine arts, acting and entertainment, music, the ministry and religious education, and public relations.

Personal Application

1. How can understanding your personality type be helpful in discovering and living your calling?
2. What are two strengths of your type? How have you used these strengths in work or volunteer ministry/service activities?
3. Based on the lists of preferences (for extravert, introvert, and so forth) in the personality type inventory, what is one weakness of your type? Who do you know personally (family members, friends, or work associates) who has a strength in the area of your weakness?

ASSESSMENT FIVE:
COMPELLING INTERESTS

Your interests are an important part of your unique design. Interests play a major role in defining who you are and shaping how you spend your time. Your interests direct your attention and therefore furnish important insights as you seek to discern your callings within work and volunteer activities.

In preparation for completing the compelling interest inventory, think about activities you like doing and subject matter you enjoy exploring and learning. Reflect on questions such as these:

- What do I do during my free time?
- Which work, leisure, and volunteer ministry/service activities have I found to be enjoyable in the past?
- Which classes have I most liked?
- Which types of magazines grab my attention?
- Which sections of a library or bookstore do I find most appealing?

Compelling Interests Inventory

Directions

1. Check off each main category (such as *Animals*) that is of interest to you.
2. Review the main categories you have checked. Choose up to five main categories of interests you would enjoy using within *work*, and record them in prioritized order in the Compelling Interests section of your Life Calling Map.
3. Now choose up to five main categories of interests that you would enjoy using within *volunteer ministry/service activities*, and record them in prioritized order on your map. (These can be the same as or different from those you recorded as work-related interests.)
4. Identify any main categories of interests that you would like to explore or develop further, and record them in prioritized order on your map. (These can be the same as or different from those you recorded previously.)
5. Identify any subcategories of particular interest (such as *dogs*) for each of the main interest categories you have recorded on your map. Sample subcategories are listed in this inventory for each main category. Feel free to write in your particular interest (such as *rescue training*) if it is not listed.

Following each of the main interest categories you have recorded on your map, write in the subcategories of interest as in the example: *Animals* (dogs, rescue training).

☐ *Animals:* dogs, cats, birds, rabbits, horses, reptiles, aquatic life, insects, wild animals, breeding, showing, training, animal care, veterinary medicine

☐ *Antiques and collectibles:* coins, currency, stamps, precious metals, collectible toys, jewelry, furniture, pottery, china, textiles, sports memorabilia, entertainment collectibles

☐ *Art:* photography, architecture, drawing, illustrating, painting, cartooning, animation, art history, art criticism, graphic arts

☐ *Books and literature:* classics, biographies, fiction, science fiction, mystery, thrillers, poetry, romance, ethnic, religious, publishing industry, bookstores, libraries

☐ *Business and money management:* leadership, management, operations, office efficiency, sales, marketing, small business, entrepreneurship, economics, corporate finance, accounting, taxes, tax preparation, investing, personal finance, real estate, international business, time management, nonprofit organizations, fund raising/development

☐ *Careers and employment:* career and life planning, job search techniques, human resources, retirement, employment law

☐ *Christianity:* Bible, church history, spiritual growth, prayer, spiritual disciplines, missions, Christian living, stewardship, church leadership, cults, apologetics, evangelism, Christian education, prophecy, spiritual warfare, theology, denominations, youth ministry, small group ministry, discipleship and mentoring, worship, Christian traditions, faith at work

☐ *Communication:* vocabulary, grammar, pronunciation, ESL (English as a second language), cross-cultural communication, etiquette, Spanish, French, Italian, Chinese, Russian, Japanese, German, Greek, Hebrew, public speaking, writing, creative writing, technical writing, grant writing, business writing, children's literature, journalism, advertising, public relations

☐ *Computers:* Internet, programming, PC applications, hardware, networking, Website design, Website maintenance, computer animation, graphic design, databases, information management, operating systems, security, e-commerce

☐ *Crafts and hobbies:* stamping, scrapbooking, glasswork, metalwork, beadwork, needlecrafts, sewing, quilting, pottery, ceramics, toymaking, miniatures, woodworking, decorative painting, flower arranging

☐ *Dance:* ballet, classical, ballroom, folk, jazz, tap, modern, popular, sacred

☐ *Diet and fitness:* dieting, weight loss, eating disorders, exercise, wellness, weight training, personal training, nutrition, aging well

☐ *Drama and performing arts:* stagecraft, acting, set design, stage makeup, scriptwriting, directing, costuming, puppetry, clowning, magic, mime, juggling, acrobatics

☐ *Education and teaching:* teaching techniques, learning styles, homeschooling, teacher training, higher education, distance education, special education, academic administration, educational guidance and counseling, curriculum design, adult education, corporate training

☐ *Energy:* electricity, hydroelectricity, solar, nuclear, fossil fuel

☐ *Engineering and construction:* chemical, structural, civil, aerospace, electrical, electronic, mechanical, building trades

☐ *Food and cooking:* entertaining, American cuisine, international cuisine, vegetarian, restaurants, meal planning, barbecuing, baking, large-quantity cooking, cooking tools and appliances

☐ *Games and humor:* chess, board games, card games, computer games, video games, word games, group activity games, children's games, therapeutic games, trivia games, comic books, cartoons, political cartoons, jokes

☐ *History:* American history, world history, ancient history, medieval history, wars

☐ *Home:* construction, remodeling and renovation, repairs, interior design and decorating, painting, wallpapering, cleaning, organizing, caretaking, hospitality

☐ *Law and judicial system:* business law, civil law, criminal law, contract law, domestic relations law, consumer protection, environmental law, human rights, immigration law, intellectual property law, ethics, wills, estates, trusts, mediation, crime, prison systems, law enforcement, forensic science

☐ *Mathematics, science, and nature:* earth science, ecology, geology, geography, environmental science, physics, mathematics, algebra, geometry, calculus, statistics, meteorology, zoology, nature, botany, chemistry, astronomy, oceanography, evolution, creationism, natural disasters, resource management

☐ *Media:* TV, radio, film, film reviews, media watchdogs, film history, classics, international films, filmmaking, screenplays, animation, celebrities, newspapers, magazines

☐ *Medicine and science:* biology, genetics, anatomy and physiology, biochemistry, biotechnology, pharmacology, medicine, treatment of injury or disease, hospitals, alternative medicine, allergies, Alzheimer's, pain, cancer, diabetes, heart disease, sleep disorders, physical disabilities, mental disabilities, women's health, men's health, medical equipment

☐ *Mental health and life issues:* counseling, psychotherapy, theories of personality, codependency, death, grief, bereavement, loss, depression, mood disorders, stress and anxiety management, eating disorders, addiction, recovery, self-esteem, anger management, fear, family violence, incest, abuse, learning disabilities, attention-deficit disorder, human development, personal growth and development, midlife transitions, aging, retirement

☐ *Music:* vocal, instrumental, songwriting, pop, rock, classical, jazz, R & B, country, opera, international, gospel, hymnody, contemporary Christian, praise, musical drama

☐ *Personal care:* make-up, hair, fashion and wardrobe, nails, personal grooming, color analysis, skin care

☐ *Plants and gardening:* landscaping, agriculture, farming, vegetables, trees, flowers, wildflowers, herbs

☐ *Politics and government:* U.S. politics, international relations, federal government, state government, local government, political activism, foreign policy, public policy, terrorism, voter registration, political campaigns, military

☐ *Relationships, parenting, and family:* pregnancy, childbirth, infertility, adoption, child rearing, child development, spiritual development of children, infants, toddlers, school-age children, teens, child care, dating, romance, marriage, weddings, sexuality, divorce, stepfamilies, single parenting, aging parents, special-needs children, elder care, care giving, grandparenting, genealogy

☐ *Religion and philosophy:* Western philosophy, Eastern philosophy, Hinduism, Buddhism, Islam, Judaism, atheism, comparative religions, New Age, spirituality (Note that *Christianity* is listed as a separate category.)

☐ *Social issues:* abortion, child abuse, spouse abuse, adoption, foster care, AIDS, sexually transmitted diseases, child care, discrimination, drug abuse, alcohol abuse, gangs, health care, homelessness, hunger, sexual issues, illegal immigration, illiteracy, pornography, poverty, teen pregnancy

☐ *Social sciences:* anthropology, archeology, sociology, cultures, human history, folklore

☐ *Sports and recreation:* football, basketball, baseball, softball, hockey, skiing, snowboarding, snowmobiling, skating, swimming, diving, walking, running, cycling, martial arts, boating, sailing, golf, tennis, horseback riding, hunting, fishing, hiking, camping, backpacking, climbing, canoeing, kayaking, rafting, scuba diving, snorkeling

☐ *Transportation and travel:* cars, car repair and restoration, classic cars, aviation, trains, railroads, ships, motorcycles, RVs, maps, U.S. travel, international travel, accommodations

Personal Application

1. Which one of your compelling interests would you most like to develop further? How might you do that?
2. Which (if any) of your top interests are you using within your current job or volunteer activities? Which would you most like to use?

ASSESSMENT SIX: SPIRITUAL GIFTS

There are different kinds of gifts, but the same Spirit.
There are different kinds of service, but the same Lord.
There are different kinds of working, but the same God
*   works all of them in all men.*
Now to each one the manifestation of the Spirit is
*   given for the common good.*   1 CORINTHIANS 12:4–7

Spiritual gifts are special abilities given to believers by the Holy Spirit, equipping them to serve and minister both within and outside of the Church, or Body of Christ. Biblical references for spiritual gifts are found in 1 Corinthians 12; Romans 12:4–8; Ephesians 4:7–16; and 1 Peter 4: 10–11. The Body of Christ needs each of our gifts. If any of us are not active in using our gifts, the Church as a whole is weakened.

Each Christian has at least one spiritual gift. Or we may have more than one gift—a "gift-mix" instead of a single spiritual gift. Discovering your gifts is a *process* of investigation, experimentation, prayer, and confirmation. Pay special attention to what types of service or ministry give you a deep sense of joy and satisfaction. Although the Bible instructs each of us to be engaged in evangelism, giving financially, and providing hospitality, a spiritual gift in areas such as these would give ability and interest beyond what is expected of every Christian.

• *How many spiritual gifts are there?* Scholars differ in the number of abilities they count as spiritual gifts. In his book *Your Spiritual Gifts Can Help Your Church Grow,* Peter Wagner states, "The Bible does not lock us into tight restrictions about the number of gifts . . . I describe 27 different spiritual gifts. This is no hard and fast number. There are probably more, there may be fewer."[1]

• *How do spiritual gifts differ from natural talents or abilities?* There often is overlap between natural abilities and spiritual gifts, but although natural abilities can be used in many ways, spiritual gifts are expressly used to carry out God's purposes. However, a good way to begin discovering your spiritual gifts is to look at the transferable skills and abilities you enjoy using in your daily life and explore whether you may have related spiritual gifts as well.

• *Are spiritual gifts given to us fully developed?* Like natural abilities, spiritual gifts develop through training and use. Someone who believes he has the gift of teaching should seek out opportunities to observe good teachers, receive training and mentoring in how to teach well, and look for opportunities to teach. He also should seek to develop his knowledge of the Bible and specific subject matter he believes God is calling him to teach.

If you think you may have a particular spiritual gift, look for some low-risk opportunities to try out using it. Even if you cannot yet do something well, you may still have a spiritual gift in that area that is ready to be developed.

• *Can an inventory tell me what my spiritual gifts are?* No inventory can give you absolute answers about your spiritual gifts because discovering your gifts is a process. It takes time, initiative, and opportunities to experiment and receive feedback from others in the Church. For example, writer and speaker Anne Graham Lotz recounts an experience early in her life when she was sitting in an audience as a Bible teacher asked them what their gifts were. She recalls her reaction:

> I silently denied having any. . . . I shrank into the shadows and did not get involved in the discussion that followed because I didn't know I had a gift, much less what it was! And I didn't know how to go about finding mine. . . .
>
> In the end, I did discover at least one of my spiritual gifts. My discovery took place several years after I learned that I had been given a gift. God had worked in my life, placing me in a position

where I had to teach His Word each week . . . to a class filled with women who had never been in a Bible study before and didn't know I couldn't teach. So week by week, I struggled with the assigned passages, doing the best I could to study and dig out the truth as God revealed it to me. And week by week the class patiently listened. In time I improved, and the class grew and multiplied until others began to describe me as a "gifted teacher."[2]

The purpose of the Spiritual Gifts Inventory is to help expedite your process of discovering and confirming your spiritual gifts. Understanding your gifts enables you to discern your calling more readily and fully.

Spiritual Gifts Inventory

Directions

1. For each spiritual gift listed, check off any sample skills and qualities (found in the second column) that describe you.
2. After reading the description of each spiritual gift, decide which of the statements—A, B, or C—is most accurate. Write the corresponding letter on the line in the first column under the name of the spiritual gift.

   A. I *do have* this spiritual gift and have used it at least once.

   B. I *may have* this spiritual gift and am interested in exploring it further.

   C. As far as I know, I *do not have* this spiritual gift at this time in my life.

   (Example: for the first spiritual gift in the table, write the letter B on the line under the word *Administration* if you think you *may have* that spiritual gift.)

   Important note: We realize that denominations and churches differ in their views on spiritual gifts. The gifts at the end of the assessment that are marked with an asterisk are ones in particular about which churches may disagree. Please complete this assessment in accordance with your own beliefs about spiritual gifts.

3. After you have completed the inventory, record on your Life Calling Map the spiritual gifts you believe you do have (those you marked with an *A*) *and* those you would like to explore further (those you marked with a *B*). (There are five lines on your map for each; if you have marked more than five gifts with an *A*, record those that you most desire to use.)

Spiritual Gift	Sample Skills and Qualities (Check Any That Apply)	Description and Biblical References
Administration _____	☐ I enjoy organizing information, people, and events. ☐ I can identify the steps needed to accomplish a particular goal or project. ☐ I tend to be task- and goal-oriented. ☐ I am good with details. ☐ I can delegate to others appropriately.	Ability to understand the goals of a small or large group, and organize information, people, and other resources to accomplish them (1 Corinthians 12:28)
Discernment _____	☐ I can perceive if a message is congruent with biblical truth. ☐ I am sensitive to spiritual energy in a person or place that is not of God. ☐ I find that my intuitive assessment of a person or situation usually tends to be proved accurate later on. ☐ I am usually able to tell whether or not an individual's motives are godly.	Ability to know whether a message or behavior that is alleged to be of God is truly of divine origin (1 Corinthians 12:8–10)
Evangelism _____	☐ I enjoy studying how to present my faith and respond to questions about Christianity. ☐ I look for opportunities to share the gospel. ☐ I am enthusiastic about sharing Jesus with others. ☐ I am able to guide people toward making a decision about becoming a Christian.	Ability to bring others to faith in Jesus Christ; passionate about presenting the gospel effectively to others (Ephesians 4:11)

Spiritual Gift	Sample Skills and Qualities (Check Any That Apply)	Description and Biblical References
Exhortation/ Encouragement ————	☐ I am focused when listening to someone. ☐ Other people often share their problems and concerns with me. ☐ I am sensitive to others' needs. ☐ I am usually able to help others see the positive elements within a difficult situation.	Ability to help others by listening attentively and providing comfort, encouragement, and wise counsel (Romans 12:6, 8)
Faith ————	☐ I feel at times that God wants to initiate something through me. ☐ I firmly believe in God's faithfulness even in the face of seemingly impossible circumstances. ☐ I am characteristically optimistic. ☐ I like helping others grow in their ability to trust God.	Ability to discern what God wants done; trusts in God to overcome apparent impossibilities; exhibits a faith that is contagious to others (1 Corinthians 12:8–9)
Giving ————	☐ I love giving generously from the resources with which God has blessed me. ☐ I seek to be a good steward of my resources so I can give more fully to God's work. ☐ I often give more than a tithe of my income. ☐ I like to motivate others to give of their resources to benefit God's kingdom.	Ability to give money or material possessions to God's work with great delight; may be rich or poor; tends to prefer giving anonymously (Romans 12:6, 8)
Helps/Service ————	☐ I enjoy being used where I am most needed. ☐ I like accomplishing specific, practical tasks. ☐ I would rather work behind the scenes than be involved in leadership. ☐ I feel I am contributing to a ministry or person by doing what needs doing.	Ability to accomplish practical and often relatively unseen tasks that support the ministries of others; tends to prefer immediate tasks more than longer-term responsibilities (1 Corinthians 12:28)

continued on the next page

Spiritual Gift	Sample Skills and Qualities (Check Any That Apply)	Description and Biblical References
Hospitality _____	☐ I enjoy making people feel welcomed and comfortable in my home and other settings. ☐ I think about the things that create an inviting and comfortable atmosphere. ☐ I am sensitive to strangers at my church and concerned that they be welcomed warmly. ☐ I enjoy attending to guests' needs.	Ability to demonstrate God's embracing love in tangible ways by offering food, lodging, and a sense of belonging to others (1 Peter 4:9–10)
Intercession _____	☐ I feel compelled to pray for the needs of others. ☐ Praying for and with others is something I enjoy and do naturally. ☐ I enjoy spending long periods of time praying. ☐ I frequently see God answering my prayers.	Ability to pray for sustained periods of time; sees many answers to prayer (there is no specific biblical text about the gift of intercession, but there is much evidence within the Body of Christ that the gift exists[3])
Knowledge _____	☐ I enjoy studying the Bible and other books to learn more about God's word. ☐ I tend to be an adept and eager learner. ☐ I enjoy spending time alone studying and developing new ideas and insights that will benefit others. ☐ I cannot always explain how I know what I know.	Ability to understand and use information to benefit the Body of Christ (1 Corinthians 12:8)
Leadership _____	☐ I am good at getting others to work together to achieve a goal. ☐ Others often look to me to provide leadership for a group of people. ☐ I am able to envision the big picture as well as the action steps needed to get there. ☐ I find that others trust the direction I set for a group or project..	Ability to set goals for the future, and to influence and direct others to accomplish God's work (Romans 12:6, 8)

Spiritual Gift	Sample Skills and Qualities (Check Any That Apply)	Description and Biblical References
Mercy	☐ I enjoy comforting and nurturing others, and conveying God's love to them one-on-one. ☐ I want to help those who are suffering emotionally, spiritually, or physically. ☐ I am able to listen to others nonjudgmentally. ☐ I am sensitive toward those who feel like outcasts and misfits.	Ability to understand and minister compassionately to those who suffer from physical, mental, or emotional problems (Romans 12:6, 8)
Shepherd/Pastor	☐ I enjoy helping others develop a mature Christian faith. ☐ I enjoy providing long-term spiritual care for a small or large group of people. ☐ I am able to determine what steps an individual should take to mature spiritually. ☐ I desire to help others find a place to use their gifts within the Body of Christ.	Ability to nurture and direct the spiritual growth of a group of believers (Ephesians 4:11)
Teaching	☐ I enjoy increasing my knowledge about the Bible and communicating biblical truths to others. ☐ People are able to understand and apply what I have taught. ☐ I desire to help others learn God's truth so that they grow in their faith and maturity. ☐ I instinctively move from learning new concepts to thinking how to present the new information to others.	Ability to comprehend and communicate biblical truths, enabling listeners to learn and apply God's Word to their lives; desires to help others know and love God (Romans 12:6–7; 1 Corinthians 12:28)
Wisdom	☐ Others seek my advice about difficult issues. ☐ I am able to listen to conflicting points of view and discern an acceptable solution or course of action.	Ability to apply spiritual knowledge and insight to specific problems and needs; consistently provides good counsel (1 Corinthians 12:8)

continued on the next page

Spiritual Gift	Sample Skills and Qualities (Check Any That Apply)	Description and Biblical References
Wisdom, *cont.*	☐ I am seen as having understanding and insight that are helpful to others in solving problems. ☐ I am able to see through complexity to the heart of a difficult matter, apply God's truths, and come up with practical solutions.	
Apostleship* _____	☐ I am motivated to share the gospel in another culture or with people who have never heard it. ☐ I am drawn to expanding ministry frontiers for the Church. ☐ I am asked to provide assistance and counsel to pastors and other leaders. ☐ I am interested in living in different places.	Ability to start new churches or ministries; may work in either one's own culture or a foreign country; possesses spiritual authority that is recognized by Christian leaders (Ephesians 4:11; see also 1 Corinthians 12:28)
Healing* _____	☐ I am sensitive to, and feel compelled to pray for, those who need some type of healing. ☐ I have seen God work through me as I prayed for someone's physical, spiritual, or emotional healing. ☐ I sense God's guidance in how I should pray for a specific person or situation. ☐ I find joy in seeing God glorified through works of healing.	Ability to be used by God to bring supernatural healing of physical, emotional, or spiritual problems (1 Corinthians 12:8–9, 28)
Miracles* _____	☐ I pray for things that are beyond normal human capabilities or not consistent with natural law. ☐ I have seen God exhibit supernatural power through me. ☐ Others have confirmed that supernatural events have occurred when I prayed.	Ability to pray for, and be used by God to bring about supernatural acts that glorify him (1 Corinthians 12:8–10, 28)

Spiritual Gift	Sample Skills and Qualities (Check Any That Apply)	Description and Biblical References
Miracles,* *cont.*	☐ I have a high degree of faith that God can and does perform miracles today.	
Prophecy*	☐ I believe God's Word is foundational for all of life. ☐ I find God gives me messages he wants conveyed to others. ☐ I am able to confront people with the truth even if what I say is difficult for people to hear. ☐ I recognize I can err, and I can accept correction when I am wrong.	Ability to declare God's truth and to proclaim how God wills things to change; wants people to align themselves with God's will (Ephesians 4:11; 1 Corinthians 12:8–10, 28)
Tongues and/or Interpretation of Tongues*	☐ I have prayed or spoken aloud in language I have never learned or heard before. ☐ I find that sometimes during times of worship or intercession I begin to speak with sounds I do not understand. ☐ I experience the Holy Spirit enabling me to understand and interpret for others the message spoken in tongues. ☐ I am able to interpret an utterance in tongues only if the Holy Spirit instructs me about that particular message.	*Tongues:* ability to receive and speak a message from God in public worship and/or pray privately in a language one has never learned. *Interpretation:* ability to explain what someone else says while speaking in tongues. (1 Corinthians 12:8–10)

Personal Application

1. What have you been taught about spiritual gifts in the past? What awareness of your spiritual gifts did you have prior to this assessment?

2. What is one action step you would like to take to explore a particular spiritual gift further?

Personal Application for Part Two

1. What benefits do you see to having completed these inventories and recorded them in your Life Calling Map?
2. Which of the six assessments was most significant for you? Why?
3. If desired, write out a prayer that expresses your gratitude for the person God has created you to be. For example:

Dear God,

I thank you for creating me in your image and designing me perfectly for the purpose you have for me to fulfill. I commit each aspect of my design—my skills, values, preferred roles, personality type, interests, and spiritual gifts—to you. I desire to live your calling for my life.

I know that your plan for my life will be accomplished only as I allow your power to flow through me. Help me to take the risks that will enable me to be a wise steward of all you have given to me. I ask you to help me live my life in such a way that I will one day hear, "Well done, good and faithful servant, enter into the joy of your Master!" Amen.

Life Calling Map for Jim Smith [Sample]

Key Scripture Verse: Micah 6:8

"What does the Lord require of you? To act justly and to love mercy and to walk humbly with your God."

★ LIFE CALLING MAP ★
MISSION STATEMENTS

Primary Calling Mission Statement

My mission is to love God with all my heart, soul, and mind, and to show his love to others in tangible ways.

Secondary Calling Mission Statements

Life Role: Husband
My mission is to love and serve my wife in practical ways; to head my family in ways that honor God; and to protect my wife, children, and home to the best of my ability.

Life Role: Father
My mission is to help my children grow up to love and serve God, and to equip them to be productive, contributing young men and women.

Life Role: Carpenter/Small Business Owner
My mission is to use my skills of construction and skilled labor, and my interests in the needs of the elderly, to adapt their homes to make their daily lives easier and safer, allowing them to be self-sufficient as long as possible.

Life Role: Church Work Day Coordinator/Member
My mission as a member of First Baptist is to worship God; to tithe and support the church; and to help maintain a beautiful and safe church campus through organizing workdays.

★ LIFE CALLING MAP ★
DIMENSIONS OF MY DESIGN [SAMPLE]

Transferable Skills

The skills I would enjoy using in a work setting are:

Assemble/Construct (P)
Operate equipment (P)
Repair/Service (P)
Provide skilled labor (P)
Calculate/Compute (D/O)
Plan (M/P)
Analyze/Evaluate (AN)
Work with financial data (D/O)

The skills I would enjoy using in a volunteer ministry/service setting are:

Assemble/Construct (P)
Repair/Service (P)
Provide skilled labor (P)
Teach/Train/Speak (H)
Work with financial data (D/O)

The skills I would like to explore or develop further are:

Mentor/Coach (H)

Skill Cluster Categories

The categories most descriptive of my areas of interest in a work setting are:

Physical (P)
Detail/Organizing (D/O)
Managing/Persuading (M/P)

The categories most descriptive of my areas of interest in a volunteer ministry/service setting are:

Physical (P)
Detail/Organizing (D/O)
Helping (H)

Core Work Values

The values most important to me in work or volunteer ministry/service activities are:

Balance
Stability
Help others
Control
Security

Preferred Roles

The roles I most prefer within work settings are:

Specialist (carpentry, cabinet making)
Caretaker (things)
Troubleshooter

The roles I most prefer within volunteer ministry/service settings are:

Caretaker (things)
Supporter/Helper
Specialist (light carpentry)

The roles I would like to explore or develop further are:

Mentor/Coach (youth)
Teacher/Trainer (hands-on skills)

Personality Type

The preferences that best describe me are:

E – Extravert
S – Sensing
T – Thinking
J – Judging

The personality traits and characteristics particularly descriptive of me are:

Like active involvement
Like to be around other people
Realistic, practical, good with details
Want to use logic and be fair
Like completing tasks
Good ability to organize tasks
Objective decision-making style

Compelling Interests

The interests I would enjoy using within work settings are:

Home (remodeling, renovation)
Business (entrepreneurship, small business growth)
Energy (solar)
Mental health and life issues (aging)

The interests I would enjoy using within volunteer ministry/service settings are:

Sports and recreation (camping, coaching youth)
Christianity (discipleship and mentoring)
Plants and gardening (landscaping)

The interests I would like to explore further are:

Food and cooking (large quantity cooking, camp food)

Spiritual Gifts

I do have this/these spiritual gift(s):

Administration
Giving
Helps/Service

The spiritual gift(s) I would like to explore further are:

Leadership

★ LIFE CALLING MAP ★
PRIORITY GOALS [SAMPLE]

Life Role: Husband

- I will take my wife out for a "date night" at least once a month beginning January, 2005.
- I will build the storage unit in the garage by March 30, 2005.

Life Role: Father

- I will build a tree house for the children by June 30, 2005.
- I will take Aaron on a special weekend trip when he turns twelve in July 2005 to discuss issues related to the teen years.

Life Role: Carpenter/Small business owner

- I will participate in a volunteer remodeling project with Rebuilding Together by August 2006.
- I will transition my business from 100 percent new construction to a 60/40 split between new construction and modifying homes for the elderly and disabled by December 1, 2006.

Life Role: Church workday coordinator/Member

- I will develop a team of at least ten people who will volunteer once a month to help maintain the church property by February 1, 2006.
- I will participate in a leadership training course at church by August 2005.

★ LIFE CALLING MAP ★
ACTION PLAN [SAMPLE]

Priority goal: I will transition my business from 100 pecent new construction to a 60/40 split between new construction and modifying homes for the elderly and disabled by December 1, 2006.

Start Date:	*End Date:*	*Action Steps:*
1/15/05	1/30/05	Research information about home modifications for elderly and disabled beginning with www.homemods.org.
1/30/05	2/6/05	Make list of most-needed home modifications; resources for developing potential customer contacts; names of local organizations and people doing this type of work.
2/15/05	2/15/05	Join and attend local chapter meeting of the National Association of the Remodeling Industry.
3/1/05	3/30/05	Conduct at least four informational interviews with people who specialize in home modifications for the elderly and disabled.
4/1/05	4/30/05	Develop business/advertising plan for transition to having 40 percent of work be modifying homes.
5/1/05	5/15/05	Develop list of prospective customers.
5/15/05	6/15/05	Schedule and conduct meetings with at least five prospective customers.
6/15/05	6/30/05	If needed, schedule meetings with additional prospective customers.

| 7/15/05 | Depends on project | Begin first modification project. |
| 7/30/05 | | Continue business development activities until modification projects represent 40 percent of my work. |

Life Calling Map for _____

Key Scripture Verse: _____

_____

_____

_____

_____

_____

★ LIFE CALLING MAP ★
MISSION STATEMENTS

Primary Calling Mission Statement

_____

_____

_____

_____

_____

_____

Secondary Calling Mission Statements

Life Role: _____

_____

_____

_____

_____

_____

_____

Life Role: _____

_____

_____

_____

_____

_____

Life Role: _____

_____

_____

_____

_____

_____

_____

Life Role: _____

_____

_____

_____

_____

_____

_____

★ LIFE CALLING MAP ★
DIMENSIONS OF MY DESIGN

Transferable Skills

The skills I would enjoy using in a work setting are:

_____

_____

_____

_____

_____

_____

_____

_____

_____

_____

The skills I would enjoy using in a volunteer ministry/service setting are:

_____

_____

_____

_____

_____

_____

_____

_____

_____

The skills I would like to explore or develop further are:

_____

_____

_____

_____

_____

Skill Cluster Categories

The categories most descriptive of my areas of interest in a work setting are:

_____

_____

_____

The categories most descriptive of my areas of interest in a volunteer ministry/service setting are:

_____

_____

_____

Core Work Values

The values most important to me in work or volunteer ministry/service activities are:

_____

_____

_____

_____

_____

Life Calling Map copyright © 2005 by Kevin and Kay Marie Brennfleck

Preferred Roles

The roles I most prefer within work settings are:

_____

_____

_____

The roles I most prefer within volunteer ministry/service settings are:

_____

_____

_____

The roles I would like to explore or develop further are:

_____

_____

_____

Personality Type

The preferences that best describe me are:

_____ – _____

_____ – _____

_____ – _____

_____ – _____

The personality traits and characteristics particularly descriptive of me are:

_____

_____

_____

_____

_____

_____

_____

_____

_____

_____

_____

_____

_____

Compelling Interests

The interests I would enjoy using within work settings are:

_____

_____

_____

_____

The interests I would enjoy using within volunteer ministry/service settings are:

_____

_____

_____

_____

The interests I would like to explore further are:

_____

_____

_____

_____

_____

Spiritual Gifts

I do have this/these spiritual gift(s):

_____

_____

_____

_____

_____

The spiritual gift(s) I would like to explore further are:

_____

_____

_____

_____

_____

★ LIFE CALLING MAP ★
PRIORITY GOALS

_____

_____

_____

_____

_____

_____

_____

_____

_____

_____

_____

_____

_____

_____

_____

_____

_____

_____

_____

_____

_____

_____

★ LIFE CALLING MAP ★
ACTION PLAN

Priority goal: _____

_____

_____

Start Date: *End Date:*   *Action Steps:*

_____   _____   _____

_____   _____   _____

_____   _____   _____

_____   _____   _____

_____   _____   _____

_____   _____   _____

_____   _____   _____

_____   _____   _____

_____   _____   _____

_____   _____   _____

_____   _____   _____

_____   _____   _____

_____   _____   _____

_____   _____   _____

_____   _____   _____

_____   _____   _____

Life Calling Map copyright © 2005 by Kevin and Kay Marie Brennfleck

PART THREE

ENVISIONING YOUR GOD-SIZED CALLING

4

PICTURING POSSIBILITIES FOR YOUR LIFE

We are limited, not by our abilities, but by our vision.   ANONYMOUS

There is no magic in small plans. When I consider my ministry, I think of the world. Anything less than that would not be worthy of Christ nor his will for my life.
                                                                    HENRIETTA MEARS

Jesus was drawing crowds. Astounded by the miraculous healings he had performed, five thousand men (plus the accompanying women and children) gathered near him by the Sea of Galilee. This man Jesus said that God was his Father and he was the promised Messiah. *What else might he say and do?* the crowd likely wondered.

The people grew hungry. Jesus was aware of their need and already had in mind what he was going to do. His plan was to meet the needs not only of their bodies but also of their hearts. A boy's humble lunch was at the centerpiece of his plan: five little barley loaves and two small pickled fish the size of sardines. The disciple Andrew brought the boy with his little sack of food to Jesus. Andrew didn't know how so little could be used. "But at least I'll let Jesus know about it," he may have reasoned.

The Bible doesn't tell us whose idea it was for the boy to give his food to Jesus. Did Andrew notice the provisions he was carrying, and suggest that the lad accompany him to Jesus? Or did the boy approach Andrew saying, "Excuse me, sir. I, uh, have some food my mother packed for me. It's not much, but could the Teacher somehow use it?"

Then Jesus took what the boy offered to him, gave thanks for it, and fed the people until they were completely satisfied. Five loaves and two fish touched with the power of God became a large enough quantity to feed every man, woman, and child, and to fill twelve baskets with leftovers as well.[1]

But what if the boy had responded differently to the situation? He could have simply opened his lunch sack with its meager contents and never thought about it being of use to Jesus. Looking at the "reality" of the situation—and not reckoning on the power of God—he might have thought, *There's nothing I can do; I may as well just eat.*

The boy in the biblical story made the choice to let go of what he had and give it to Jesus. He didn't know what would happen. He didn't know if he would be left hungry. By relinquishing what he had, however, he unleashed the power of God and found himself positioned at the very center of a miracle.

Your Own Loaves and Fishes

Your Life Calling Map identifies key puzzle pieces of your God-given design. In a very real way, they are *your* loaves and fishes. God wants to use them; in fact, he has given them to you for specific purposes in his great plan. The boy was willing to hand over his lunch because he saw something in Jesus that inspired trust. Are you ready—and willing—to entrust your gifts to God for his use? If you do, you might very well find miraculous things happening in your own life.

One of the keys to living your calling is enlarging your perspective of how God wants to use your life, allowing yourself to envision a "God-sized" calling. Such a calling is one that you cannot accomplish with your own power and resources. A God-sized calling, by definition, requires God's power and resources to succeed. In the next two chapters you will find many tools and resources for discovering how you can partner with God to use your gifts in your family, your neighborhood, your career, your church, your community, and the world at large.

The Power of Vision

Bill Hybels took the board of directors of Willow Creek Community Church to visit some inner-city ministries for which the church was providing funding and volunteers. He recounts standing with them in a hot, empty, humid warehouse. The person leading the ministry soon took their minds off the discomfort, however, as he began to describe for Hybels and the others his vision for the space.

"Imagine that corner of this warehouse filled with electrical supplies. A skilled worker from a church could stop here, pick up all the supplies he or she needs, then go over to the home of someone in need and fix the wiring."

Enthusiastically, he then asked them to imagine pallets stacked with drywall compound that would be used to patch holes in the homes of those who couldn't afford to fix them. Pointing to another part of the warehouse, he described the high stacks of blankets that would occupy it to help people keep warm in the winter when their homes have no heat.

Hybels said he was reaching for his wallet in response to the power of the man's godly vision.[2]

Vision, as we are using the term, refers to the God-given ability to picture things in our minds that are not yet reality. A man sees an empty warehouse full of goods that can provide help and hope to people. A couple envision opening their home to foster children. A college student visualizes herself treating patients after completing her education to become a doctor. A woman pictures how her artistic gifts could be used to bring hope to children in a low-income neighborhood. A vision is a picture or idea of how God could use your gifts and your life to meet needs and accomplish his purposes.

"Christian vision," explains Os Guinness, ". . . is inspired directly or indirectly by the call of God. It is an act of imaginative seeing that combines the insight of faith, which goes to the heart of things below the surface, and the foresight of faith, which soars beyond the present with the power of a possible future. This combining of the not-yet-combined is the secret of visionary faith. . . . Dreamers of the day come into their own and stay on course when they follow the calling of Christ."[3]

God-inspired visions of your calling always have doing the work of God's kingdom as their ultimate goal. As Andy Stanley says, "God's ultimate plan for your life reaches beyond the visions he's given you for your family, business, ministry, and finances. He has positioned you in your culture as a singular point of light. A beacon in a world that desperately needs to see something divine, something that is clearly not of this world."[4]

Steps of Faith

Many of us live as though we are waiting for God to send us his vision for our life via fax, e-mail, or a supernatural revelation—spelling out the actions we are to take in step-by-step detail. We also may want this divine message to include an ironclad guarantee that we will be safe from risk, financially secure, and successful in others' eyes as we carry out this heavenly plan for our lives.

The problem with this expectation is that God doesn't usually choose to work this way. Rather, we see in the lives of great people of faith, the journeys of our clients, and in our own lives that God often calls his people by creating a mental image or compelling idea of how our gifts can be used to meet needs in the world. The vision gives enough direction for us to step out in obedience and faith, but it doesn't give all the details or provide guarantees about the outcome.

The story of James Dobson and his founding of Focus on the Family exemplifies how a God-sized calling can begin. Today, the nonprofit organization has a multitude of ministries, including Dobson's internationally syndicated radio programs, which are heard daily on more than three thousand radio stations in the United States and more than ninety-five other countries. Its magazines reach millions of households. The organization has had, and continues to have, an enormous impact on people throughout the world.

It all started as a God-inspired vision in the mind of a man who was willing to be used. "I wish I could say that I knew where the Lord was leading when I started Focus on the Family, but that is not true," said Dobson. "I simply felt He wanted me to prepare a regular broadcast and to speak to family-related issues." So he stepped out in faith, renting a tiny office in Arcadia, California, to begin his radio program. "Everything that has happened since then has been a surprise and a labor of love."[5]

Most of us will not be called to develop and lead an international organization. God-sized visions can be of differing dimensions and degrees of visibility. God might call one person to develop a new worldwide evangelism ministry that has an impact on millions; he might call another to start an outreach Bible study in her neighborhood. In one person God might instill a vision for a nonprofit organization that uses innovative ways to collect food in the community and distribute it to local ministries. In another person, the vision God plants may be one of making his church's food bank more organized, efficient, and effective.

Size in the world's terms isn't what is important. For a calling to be God-sized, it simply has to be a vision that depends on God's power and resources to succeed. Resist comparing your calling to that of anyone else. God holds you accountable only for using the gifts and opportunities he has given to you. God judges us according to the degree of our obedience, not according to the size of our dreams.

A Vision Unfolds

Regardless of the size or scope of your callings, however, you are likely to experience uncertainty as you respond to God's leading. Jesus called his disciples with the words, "Follow me." He didn't give them a detailed explanation of all that would be involved. Similarly, visions of your callings will unfold and become clearer only as you move forward in pursuing them.

The vision of our own vocational calling began with an interest in helping people expand their vision of what they could do with their lives.

We were intrigued with people's giftedness and wanted to help them recognize and use their gifts meaningfully in the world. We dreamed of being catalysts for people discovering and living the lives God created them to live. Our interest grew into a passion that led us to our calling.

On January 31, 1987, about eighteen months before we married, we led our first workshop together at our church. Sixteen participants joined us that day to engage in looking at the topic "Heart's Desires: Making God's Dreams for You Come True." Four of those participants became Kevin's first career counseling clients for his new private practice. Although we didn't realize it at the time, that Saturday marked the beginning of a significant new chapter in our journey of discovering and living our calling. As is often the case, we had little idea of what God had in store for us.

For several years, Kevin had envisioned starting some type of center to help people use their gifts and abilities more fully, and dare dreaming God-sized dreams. His vision eventually led to founding our career and life planning firm, Lifework Design, which became widely known in the Christian community in our area. We had the privilege of serving thousands of people through individual career counseling, workshops, seminars, and outplacement services.

In 1997 we launched our first Website (www.ChristianCareerCenter. com), which expanded our impact from our local area to around the world. It has allowed us to work with clients throughout the United States as well as from Canada, Europe, Asia, and Africa. Currently receiving more than one million hits per month, it has exposed countless people to articles and other resources for becoming the people God created them to be and doing the things he designed them to do.

We have learned that the path our calling takes us on is usually not predictable or wholly foreseeable. In 1987, when we held our first workshop, for example, we knew nothing about the Internet. But God knew and had already planned how he would use it in our lives and for the advancement of his kingdom. As we write these words, we don't know how God will choose to use us in the future. We are certain, however, that he will lead us on an adventure even greater than we can envision.

God-Driven Visions

A vision of what God is calling you to do may start as an interest, a tiny idea, or a fleeting thought. It can be inspired by a variety of catalysts:

• *It might be need-driven.* An individual sees a need that he or she wants to help meet. After almost twenty years in aerospace, Michael decided he wanted to use his computer skills for a new purpose. He became interested in Wycliffe Bible Translators (WBT) and its mission to translate the New Testament for each language group.

Wanting to help meet the needs of the three hundred million people who do not yet have God's Word in their own language, Michael and his family joined WBT in 1996. They are part of a team whose mission is "using computers to speed Bible translation." They call themselves "technicianaries; missionaries who provide technical knowledge and skills to make tools needed by other missionaries."[6] Michael's ability to envision innovative uses of technology has allowed him to make significant contributions to Wycliffe's mission of putting the Bible into everyone's hand in his or her own language.

• *It might be design-driven.* A person begins picturing possibilities or looking for opportunities to use particular puzzle pieces of his or her design (such as skills, interests, or preferred roles). Laura's strong interest and skills in writing and editing were both the motivation and the means for moving out of the secretarial field.

Her initial endeavors in writing an article for a church publication and doing freelance proofreading for a monthly newsletter have led to numerous writing and editing projects for Christian organizations and publishers. Laura recently achieved her goal of being a published author when her story was chosen for a special anthology of essays about mothers.

• *It might be experience-driven.* A person has had a particular life experience and wants to help others who are going through the same thing. Barbara was finishing chemotherapy when she began career counseling to help her figure out what she might want to do next in her life. For several years, she had been interested in helping women with various life issues. Her experience with cancer intensified a desire to create a place in which women could find resources, seminars, and counseling for a variety of needs.

Barbara has targeted founding a nonprofit women's center within five years. In preparation, she is working on a graduate degree in counseling. She is also speaking to women's groups on what cancer has taught her—such as the truth that life is too short to waste it doing things that don't count for eternity.

The stimulus for a vision can be a combination of factors, of course. The important point is that your vision of a calling can originate in any number of ways. All of these catalysts for a vision of using your gifts in the world can be *God-driven*. God is creative, often surprising us in how he works in our lives. "As workers for God we have to learn to make room for God—to give God 'elbow room,'" entreats Oswald Chambers. "Keep your life so constant in its contact with God that His surprising power may break out on the right hand and on the left. Always be in a state of expectancy, and see that you leave room for God to come in as He likes."[7]

God asks us to take the puzzle pieces of our design and entrust them to him to be used and multiplied. As we relinquish our gifts to God, we can expect him to be at work in our lives, helping us envision how we can use our gifts in our work, church, home, neighborhood, community, and the world. The visions that God creates in our hearts and minds are always beyond what we feel is possible. As Andy Stanley says, "The task always appears to be out of reach. And the reason it appears that way is because it is. God-ordained visions are always too big for us to handle. We shouldn't be surprised. Consider the source."[8]

Personal Application

1. What is your reaction to the idea of a God-sized calling—that is, something larger than what you can accomplish within your own power?
2. Describe a time when you had a vision (picture, idea) of something you could do that was need-driven, design-driven, or experience-driven. What did you do? What was the result?

5

TOOLBOX OF STRATEGIES FOR STRETCHING YOUR VISION

Never concede to doing something so small that it could be accomplished entirely in your lifetime.
                                                                            RALPH WINTER

One day Michelangelo walked into the studio of Raphael and looked at one of his early drawings. He took a piece of chalk and wrote across the drawing *Amplius,* meaning "greater" or "larger." Michelangelo saw the plan of the gifted artist as being too cramped and narrow.

Similarly, perhaps God looks down on our plans for our lives today and, knowing what he can do through us, longs to write over our plans, "Amplius! Greater! Larger!"[1]

This chapter presents a toolbox of strategies for widening your perspective about career and volunteer options. The strategies are designed to help you enlarge your vision of possible ways God could use you in the world. Identifying several possible ideas enables you to make better decisions about how to use your skills, interests, and abilities.

Widening Tunnel Vision

Tunnel vision refers to having a limited view of available choices. Most of us have been exposed to only a small percentage of the thousands of career and volunteer possibilities that exist. Our vision of the world of work typically is confined to jobs held by family members and friends, those we have personally observed, and careers to which we are exposed in the media. Therefore we are unaware of other opportunities that could be a good fit for our design.

People often begin career counseling with no idea of which new career they want to pursue. From their past work experience and jobs they have seen others do, they know what they *don't* want to do, but they draw a blank when it comes to identifying what they *do* want to do. Sensing their tunnel vision, they may say, "I need to know what else is out there." We observe a similar pattern as we help people find places they can serve in their churches or communities.

The process of envisioning possibilities moves people from having a mental question mark about work and volunteer activities to developing a list of intriguing alternatives. In addition, when a person already has an idea of what he or she might want to do, generating and comparing options helps clarify if the original idea is the best choice.

Strategies for Stretching Your Vision

Norman Vincent Peale said, "To achieve anything significant, everyone needs a little imagination and a big dream." Most of us have "dreaming muscles" that are rather underdeveloped and could use a little exercise. Too often, we either don't dare to dream at all or let ourselves dream only "safe" dreams we know are achievable within our own power. It is no wonder our lives often lack power and excitement!

The Bible tells us in Luke 1:37, "For nothing is impossible with God." God is all-powerful and owns all the resources in the world. We who claim to know and serve him should be the biggest dreamers of all. These exercises will help you stretch your vision to see new ways God can use your gifts in the world.

Strategy One: Envisioning Your God-Empowered Life

Using your Life Calling Map: Dimensions of My Design, stretch your dreaming muscles and come up with at least three responses to this question: Since all things are possible with God, and he can supply everything I need, in what exciting ways can I use my God-given gifts to meet needs in the world?

Strategy Two: Envisioning Possibilities Through Brainstorming

In this exercise, you brainstorm (generate ideas) about work and volunteer ministry/service options with your partner or small group. Brainstorming helps you connect the puzzle pieces of your design in new ways. If you have found in the past that brainstorming on your own is challenging, you will enjoy seeing how this exercise taps into the creative power of others. You may find your own creativity stimulated, as well.

• Arrange a time for you and your partner or Live Your Calling Group to have a brainstorming session. (It is session five of the twelve-week Live Your Calling Small Group Guide, which is found in Appendix A.) If you have not been working with a partner or group, you can invite one or more people to get together to brainstorm with you.

• Schedule enough time so that each person has at least fifteen or twenty minutes for the group to focus on him or her. (More time is even better.) You may want to have a timer that signals when each person's time is up so that no one gets shortchanged. Consider having pizza or dessert during your brainstorming meeting; good food can increase creativity!

• Have each person bring enough photocopies of the transferable skills and compelling interests results from his or her Life Calling Map so that each person in the group can look at them during the brainstorming session.

• Taking each person in turn, the group comes up with as many ideas as possible for work and volunteer activities that would use one or more transferable skills and one or more compelling interests. (An example follows these directions.) Although your group doesn't have to proceed in an organized fashion, it is sometimes helpful at least to begin with a little structure. For example, take each transferable skill and brainstorm how it can be combined with each of the compelling interests.

Here are some additional suggestions for your brainstorming session:

- Piggyback on others' ideas. Use their ideas to trigger your own thinking.
- Avoid using job titles, because it limits the brainstorming to known jobs. Instead of someone saying "You could be an *architect*," he could say, "You could *design* homes."
- Don't judge or evaluate your own or others' ideas. Negativity can destroy creativity. As people are giving you ideas, refrain from saying anything like "I could never see myself doing that" or giving your group a look that says, "You have got to be kidding!" Instead, remain neutral, accepting and writing down all the ideas people give you.
- During your turn, you contribute ideas as well as write down each brainstormed idea in your notebook or journal. If there is time after everyone has taken a turn, take five minutes, have people review their lists, and mark the ideas that are most interesting. Give each person a minute or two to share a few ideas of particular interest.

Here is an example of ideas from a brainstorming session:

- Brainstorming question: *How could these compelling interests be combined with any of the transferable skills in work or volunteer ministry/service activities?*
- Sample compelling interests: sports and recreation—backpacking, camping, rock climbing
- Sample transferable skills: design/create, mentor/coach; plan
- Sample brainstormed ideas

  Plan backpacking trips for youth groups
  Plan rock climbing trips for adventure travel group
  Plan outdoor trips for disabled people
  Lead outdoor trips that promote spiritual growth
  Lead team-building backpacking trips
  Design backpacking equipment

Take juvenile offenders on camping trips

Plan and run youth day camps during summer

Lead rock-climbing trips in national parks

Design and build rock-climbing parks

Create displays in recreation equipment stores

Help others plan for their outdoor adventures

Strategy Three: Discovering Volunteer Opportunities in Your Church and Community

The first step in picturing how you might become involved in your local church or community is finding out what opportunities already exist *and* what opportunities might be created. Here are some suggestions for you and your partner or small group.

At your church: Find out if any lists of ministries and opportunities for involvement already exist.

Call the church office, ask the pastor(s) and directors of various ministries (children's, men's, women's ministries, and so on), look at printed information that is on display at church, and read through your church's Website.

Talk to people who head departments or ministries to find out more about what is going on in your church. (This is especially important if there is little written information.) In addition to finding out what opportunities already exist, ask them what ideas, dreams, and plans they have that are not yet happening. What do they need to enlarge, change, or improve?

You can also find out what is happening in other churches that interests you. Perhaps there is something similar happening in your church already, or maybe God wants to use you to get a new ministry or activity started.

In your community: Finding volunteer opportunities of interest in your community may take some resourcefulness. Here are some ideas to get you started:

Do an Internet search for "volunteer opportunities" and the name of your city (example: volunteer opportunities + Boston, MA).

Look under Social Services in your local Yellow Pages.

Contact the chamber of commerce.

Ask a reference librarian for resources.

Ask at your church or school for suggestions.

Then see if you and your partner(s) can each find (or create) at least two volunteer activities of interest. Here is a list of sample church ministry and community service activities to stimulate your thinking. (Where applicable, we have added the primary skill cluster category: P = physical; AN = analytical; CR = creative; H = helping; M/P = managing/persuading; and D/O = detail/organizing—that the activity would use.)

- Create an aesthetically pleasing environment by providing landscaping or gardening assistance to churches or nonprofit organizations. (P)
- Help prepare mailings or weekly church bulletins. (D/O)
- Provide medical care and health education to the church family or the local community. (H, AN)
- Assist a church or nonprofit agency with its computer activities, such as Website development and maintenance, database administration, database development, networking, general programming, and so on. (AN)
- Organize the office or files for a church or nonprofit organization to increase efficiency. (D/O)
- Use skills in illustration, graphic arts, or photography to help produce bulletins, banners, posters, newsletters, and so forth that promote events and create a sense of excitement about various opportunities. (CR)
- Serve as a lay counselor to people, offering healing assistance to those experiencing personal, marital, or family need. (H)
- Operate video, lighting, or audio equipment during services or other programs and events. (P)
- Write daily devotions for a church Website to promote the reading of God's Word and spiritual growth. (CR)
- Assist the church or organization's leaders with strategic planning for the future. (M/P, AN)
- Help others use their financial resources wisely by teaching money management skills. (M/P)

- Provide practical assistance to the elderly (light housecleaning, yard work, transportation to stores, handling correspondence, doctor appointments, church). (P, H, D/O)
- Offer free car repair services for low-income families. (P)

Strategy Four: Envisioning Career Possibilities Using Career Resources

The *Occupational Information Network* database *(O*NET)* and the *Occupational Outlook Handbook (OOH)* are two career resources that are helpful tools for finding work options that fit your design. They can also be helpful in stimulating your thinking about volunteer activities of interest. However, without your Life Calling Map these resources can seem overwhelming. Your map helps direct you to the most important areas to explore.

The resources can be accessed online (the *OOH* is also available in print). The *O*NET OnLine* database is found at http://online.onetcenter.org and the *OOH* is on our Website (www.ChristianCareerCenter.com, in the Career Exploration section). We suggest beginning with the *O*NET,* which is a database that includes descriptions for about 1,000 jobs, and then using the *OOH,* which has more extensive information about the 250 jobs that are held by approximately 85 percent of the American workforce.

Like many of our clients, you may find that these resources lead you to a great career that fits your design. Jack worked in the hotel industry for a number of years but wanted to do something that allowed him to help people in a more direct way. While reading through the *OOH,* he came across the description for occupational therapist and was surprised at how well it fit his Life Calling Map. Today, as an occupational therapist, he is helping stroke victims regain skills and confidence in their daily lives.

Your goal in using the *O*NET* is to identify several jobs you would like to explore further. The *O*NET* database contains lists of job titles that have been organized into "job family" categories. Table 5.1 helps you determine which job family categories relate to the skill cluster categories you recorded on your Life Calling Map.

TABLE 5.1. HOW THE *O*NET* CATEGORIES RELATE TO THE SKILL CLUSTER CATEGORIES.

Skill Cluster Categories (from Your Life Calling Map)	Related *O*NET* Job Families
Physical (P)	• Architecture & Engineering • Arts, Design, Entertainment, Sports & Media • Building and Grounds Cleaning & Maintenance • Construction & Extraction • Education, Training & Library • Farming, Fishing & Forestry • Food Preparation & Serving Related • Healthcare Support • Installation, Maintenance & Repair • Life, Physical & Social Sciences • Management • Military Specific • Personal Care & Service • Production • Protective Service • Transportation & Material Moving
Analytical (AN)	• Architecture & Engineering • Computer & Mathematical • Education, Training & Library • Healthcare Practitioners & Technical • Life, Physical & Social Sciences • Military Specific
Creative (CR)	• Architecture & Engineering • Arts, Design, Entertainment, Sports & Media • Education, Training & Library • Food Preparation & Serving Related
Helping (H)	• Community & Social Services • Education, Training & Library • Food Preparation & Serving Related • Healthcare Practitioners & Technical • Healthcare Support • Life, Physical & Social Sciences • Management • Personal Care & Service
Managing/Persuading (M/P)	• Business & Financial Operations • Legal • Management • Military Specific • Personal Care & Service • Sales and Related

continued on the next page

**TABLE 5.1. HOW THE *O*NET CATEGORIES RELATE
TO THE SKILL CLUSTER CATEGORIES,** *continued.*

Skill Cluster Categories (from Your Life Calling Map)	Related *O*NET Job Families
Detail/Organizing (D/O)	• Business & Financial Operations • Computer & Mathematical • Education, Training & Library • Healthcare Practitioners & Technicians • Healthcare Support • Legal • Life, Physical & Social Sciences • Military Specific • Office & Administrative Support • Personal Care & Service • Protective Service • Sales and Related

Using the *O*NET, you can review more detailed information about a wide variety of jobs and compare that information with the information about your design in your Life Calling Map. We suggest that you take brief notes about any job that is of some interest to you. Table 5.2 gives a suggested worksheet format to use. You will find more detailed information about how to use the *O*NET and *OOH* in Appendix B.

TABLE 5.2. WORKSHEET FOR EVALUATING JOB OPTIONS.

Job Title, *O*NET*-SOC Code, and *O*NET* Job Family	Aspects of the Job That Seem to Fit My Design	Aspects of the Job That Do Not Seem to Fit My Design	Questions or Comments
Advertising and Promotions Manager, 11-2011.00 (Management)	• *Use creativity in planning ad campaigns* • *Lots of people contact* • *Make presentations and do training*	• *Work with budgets*	*How much negotiation is involved in this job? What is an entry level job in this area?*

Personal Application

1. Across which parts of your life might God want to write "Amplius! Greater! Larger!"?
2. Do vision stretching strategy two with your partner or Live Your Calling Group.
3. Complete at least one additional vision stretching strategy.
4. Make a list of the most interesting work and volunteer options.
5. If desired, write a prayer asking God to guide you as you work with these envisioning and exploration activities. Here is an example:

> Dear God,
>
> Thank you for your love, faithfulness, and complete trustworth-iness. Thank you for choosing to involve me in your work in the world. Help me to envision the tasks you have chosen for me. Guide me in joyfully seeing ways of using my gifts in the world.
>
> Help me to participate with the work of your Spirit within me, removing any blocks to seeing what you have created me to be and to do. Sensitize me to the needs you have designed me to serve in this world. Help me dare to create visions that are much bigger than myself. Enable me to submit to your power, to be stretched, challenged, and transformed into the person you desire me to be. Amen.

6

TOOLBOX OF STRATEGIES FOR TESTING YOUR VISIONS

Buy the truth and do not sell it; get wisdom,
discipline and understanding.   PROVERBS 23:23

Face reality as it is, not as you wish it to be.   *PETER KOESTENBAUM*

Have you ever been in a job that felt more like a prison sentence than a calling? Sometimes we find ourselves in the wrong type of work because we made a career decision on the basis of our *perception* of a job instead of its *reality.* Our image of a job is shaped by many factors, including how particular careers are portrayed on TV and in movies.

The TV show *LA Law* (which ran from 1986 to 1994) was a prime example of the media's powerful impact on how people view particular jobs and their subsequent career choices. The show depicted the personal and professional lives of a group of attorneys in Los Angeles. Their workdays were packed with drama, excitement, and romance. They drove high-performance cars and owned multimillion-dollar homes. Many viewers were apparently motivated by the show to pursue a career in law. A major university reported an astonishing 400 percent increase in law school applications after *LA Law* came on the air! Reality testing probably came years later during their first weeks as an attorney, when they discovered that their jobs bore little resemblance to those portrayed on *LA Law.*

At one time or another, many of us have found ourselves in a job that ended up being very different from our initial picture of it. We may have discovered belatedly that we lacked a realistic understanding of the job or career before entering it. Our inaccurate image of the job might have been due to not taking the time—or not knowing how—to check it out thoroughly beforehand.

Students, for example, may base their career choices solely on classes they enjoyed ("I liked my psychology courses, so I think I'll become a counselor"). Yet the work of a therapist—and the reality of making a living in the field—is quite different from studying psychology. Conversely, a person can dismiss a particular field of study that could lead to a well-fitting job because of a negative learning experience. So even though an enjoyable high school or college course can be the beginning point of an interest in a career field, classes alone do not yield sufficient information to make a career decision.

Many other factors can influence us to make career decisions that don't fit who we are:

- Pressure from family or others to pursue a particular career path
- The lure of hot jobs and a large salary
- Taking what is offered because we don't know what else to do
- Thinking that the professional ministry is the only place we can serve God

The strategies in this chapter help you choose a career path that feels like a calling rather than a prison sentence.

Strategies for Reality Testing Your Options

In the last chapter, you developed a list of potential career and volunteer ministry/service choices. Reality testing means thoroughly checking them out ahead of time. Asking questions, reading, observing, investigating, volunteering, and trying things out all enable you to see how well particular activities and work environments fit your design *before* committing yourself to a job or educational program. The purpose of the four strategies presented here is to help you gather enough in-depth information to ensure that you have a realistic picture of each option.

Strategy One: Using Career-Specific Resources to Gather Information

There is a wealth of career-specific resources available in your local bookstore and library. They can help you gain insider's information about specific career fields and industries. Here are a couple of examples:

- One extensive line of career books that our clients have particularly liked is the *VGM Careers for You Series,* that includes titles such as *Careers for Sports Nuts and Other Athletic Types, Careers for Good Samaritans and Other Humanitarian Types, Careers for Puzzle Solvers and Other Methodical Types,* plus more than thirty others.
- There are many resources for people interested in self-employment. Paul and Sarah Edwards, for example, have written many helpful books in this area, among them *Best Home Businesses for the 21st Century, The Entrepreneurial Parent,* and *Making Money with Your Computer at Home.* For those interested in purchasing a business, *Entrepreneur* magazine rank-orders the top 500 franchises each year (see www.Entrepreneur.com for more information). The Small Business Administration (www.sba.gov) and SCORE (or Service Corps of Retired Executives, "Counselors to America's Small Businesses"; www.score.org) also offer many helpful resources.

There are specialized resources available for all career fields. Whether you are interested in working in the government, nonprofit agencies, higher education, a technical field, a creative field, the ministry, or elsewhere, you can find good information that enables you to discern better how well specific career alternatives fit you. Ask your local reference librarian or bookstore clerk or use the search function on a Website that sells books. In-depth and interesting information is out there for you to find and use.

Strategy Two: Using Professional Associations to Gather Information

A professional association is an organization of people with shared interests. It creates a forum for networking and exchanging information and ideas. An association can also be a key source of information for people investigating specific career fields and industries. Professional associations are not just for white-collar jobs. There are associations for locksmiths, car wash operators, fishermen, arts and craftspeople, and sled dog racers. With more than twenty thousand professional associations, there is one for almost every interest.

The Encyclopedia of Associations is the premier resource for finding the professional organizations that represent fields of interest to you. It is a three-volume set of reference books, available in most libraries. A person interested in financial planning, for example, would find more than fifteen professional organizations. Each association's listing includes contact information, Website address, and a description of what the association does. The *Occupational Outlook Handbook* (found in the Career Exploration portion of our Website, www.ChristianCareerCenter.com) also lists professional associations under "Sources for Additional Information."

Professional associations can help you explore careers in several ways. They may offer pamphlets, books, and other information. They can connect you with a local chapter of the association, where you can learn more about the profession and develop personal contacts. Many associations also furnish listings of job openings on their Websites.

For many clients, professional associations have been the key to a successful career transition. Shelly was interested in making a living doing what she found herself doing for free: organizing other people's homes and offices for them. She found the National Association of Professional Organizers (NAPO) (http://www.napo.net/) through using the *Encyclopedia of Associations* and connected with the local chapter. They invited her to attend a chapter meeting, during which she made several contacts and learned a lot about the business of professional organizing. A few months later, she successfully launched her own business.

Strategy Three: Informational Interviewing and Shadowing

Reading books and information on Websites is an efficient way of learning more about specific careers and narrowing down your list of alternatives. Once you have learned what you can through written information, it is time to gather some live information by talking to people who are doing the types of work or volunteer activities of interest to you. This is called informational interviewing.

Informational interviewing is an invaluable method of gathering information beyond what you can find in written resources. It also is a means of learning about jobs that you have not been able to find described in written resources. We recommend that you do a minimum of three informational interviews in different settings (that is, not all in the same organization) for any job you are considering seriously.

Informational interviewing also results in developing a contact network. Bill was interested in moving from banking to the field of development in nonprofit organizations. His informational interviewing contacts helped him land an internship through which he learned about the field firsthand and gained experience he could list on his resume.

Here are some sample questions for an informational interview:[1]

- What are a typical day's (week's) activities in your job?
- How did you get involved in this field?
- What do you enjoy most about your work?
- What do you enjoy least about your work?
- What is a typical salary range in this profession?
- What steps would I need to take to enter this type of work?
- Could you suggest two or three other people with whom I could talk about this type of work?

Shadowing goes a step beyond information interviewing. This refers to spending time in a particular work environment, watching one or more people do their jobs. You can learn more about the specifics of a job and also observe the physical work environment.

Pat's story illustrates the exciting things that can result from making connections with people in a field of interest. While exploring several careers, she became interested in jewelry making. She conducted informational interviews with jewelers in three stores. As a means of getting her foot in the door, she later used her background as an administrative assistant to get hired for a customer service job in one of them.

While working in the store, she learned about their jeweler apprentice program. After she took a hands-on "bench test," the master jeweler called Pat a natural and accepted her into the apprentice program. She says, "I can't put into words how happy I am. I look forward to getting to work, and each day flies by. My former customer service coworkers are within my field of vision in the shop and they keep kidding me about my constant grin while I'm working."

Strategy Four: Trying It Out

If you are primarily interested in exploring volunteer ministry/service activities, this strategy is probably the most appropriate and helpful. Typically, volunteer positions give you the opportunity to drop in and drop out with little difficulty, cost, or risk. Trying out a number of volunteer activities at a church or other nonprofit organization is a terrific way to explore your gifts and interests, develop new skills, and meet new people.

For those of you who are seeking your calling in work, this strategy may or may not be necessary. Using the previous strategies, you may have gathered all the information you need for making your career decision. However, there are times when you will want to invest more time and energy in exploring a particular career through hands-on involvement.

You can gain experience through volunteering your services (for a few hours, weeks, or months), participating in an internship (sometimes you can even earn college credits while doing this), and serving in a position at a church or nonprofit agency.

If you are interested in trying something out, you may have to take the initiative to find the right opportunity. Ask your informational interview contacts if there are (or could be) volunteer opportunities at their workplace. Ask your family members and friends if they know of people or organizations you could contact to inquire about volunteer situations or internships. Call local organizations and companies and inquire about opportunities. Contact professional organizations to inquire about volunteer or internship opportunities. Ask your college's career center or your professors for suggestions. Ask your pastor about opportunities in your church or denomination where you could test your vision or try out using particular skills. You will never know what is possible until you ask!

The Value of Reality Testing

Using the vision testing strategies enables you to develop an accurate understanding of how well various alternatives fit your design *before* making a decision about which to pursue. Testing your vision of a particular career or volunteer pursuit can help you discern whether it is something God is calling you to do. Your research can also help you be more successful in your vocational calling because you will know what is required to excel. The book of Proverbs exhorts us to get wisdom and understanding; reality testing helps you to do so as you seek to invest your gifts wisely in this world.

Personal Application

1. How did you choose your current or most recent job? Did you do any reality testing prior to making your choice? If so, what did you do?
2. Complete the vision testing strategies, which help you accomplish your goals for using this book:

   If you want to identify career options, we recommend that you complete strategies one and three to start (and the others, if needed).

   If you want to identify volunteer ministry/service possibilities, we recommend beginning with three or four.
3. Develop a list of the three to five career and/or volunteer options that seem to fit your Life Calling Map: Dimensions of My Design best.

4. Evaluate how God-sized each option on your list appears to be. Give each option a ranking from 1 to 5:

    1 = Totally "me-sized"; I'm confident I could do this with my own abilities and resources.

    3 = Somewhat God-sized; I have some doubts that I could do this on my own.

    5 = Totally God-sized; the only way I could do this would be if God provides the resources I need.

PART FOUR

MAKING DECISIONS
WITHIN THE WILL OF GOD

7

PARTNERING WITH GOD
IN DECISION MAKING

Guidance is largely consecrated and sanctified thinking.   JAMES JAUNCY

H ow do I know what God is calling me to do?" asked Jim, looking
at a list of options. His brainstorming and exploration of various
careers had yielded three possibilities he found particularly interesting.
"I could envision myself doing any of these. So how do I know which
is my calling?" He paused and then added, "And how would I know if
God wants me to do something that isn't even on my list?"

When we come to the point of making decisions about our callings
within work or other important life roles, we may find ourselves asking questions such as these: Shouldn't finding my calling be a mysteri-
ous spiritual experience instead of a systematic process? Can it really
be a calling if it is something I have decided to do instead of something
to which God has supernaturally directed me? Questions of this kind
stem in part from our difficulty in knowing how to find a balance between the human and the divine.

In Chapter One, we differentiated between the two types of callings that God, the Caller, extends to us. Our primary calling is an invitation to an ongoing relationship with God through faith in Jesus Christ.
When the Bible uses the term *calling*, it refers to our primary calling (as in

Ephesians 4:1). Scripture gives a clear description of what this calling is, how we can respond to it, and what we need to do to live it.

In contrast, the Bible does not give us definitive instructions about our secondary calling to work (whether paid or unpaid). It does not give us specific answers about which career path we should choose or volunteer opportunities we should undertake. Instead, the Bible gives us *principles* for making decisions within God's will.

Many of us struggle with knowing what to do when we face an important decision about our callings. We may wrestle with knowing if it is up to God to guide or up to us to decide. The key to resolving this dilemma is realizing that it is both: God promises to guide *and* we are called to decide.

Called to Be a Decision Maker

God certainly can indicate supernaturally which job or career path we should pursue. At times, he may choose to do so. More typically, however, he calls us to take responsibility for making good decisions about how to use our gifts in the world. Dallas Willard counsels that ". . . in general, it is God's will that we ourselves should have a great part in determining our path through life. . . . God both *develops* and, for our good, *tests* our character by leaving us to decide. He calls us to responsible citizenship in his kingdom by saying—in effect or in reality—as often as possible, 'My will for you in this case is that you decide on your own.'"[1]

In the absence of direct supernatural guidance, we need to assume that God wants us to decide prayerfully and thoughtfully which work or volunteer alternative is the best choice. "It is possible to pray, read God's Word, seek counsel, and still not feel led by God," says Bruce Waltke. "That's the time to rely on sound judgment. God gave each of us a brain, and He expects us to put it to good use."[2]

Scripture illustrates that even biblical superstars such as the Apostle Paul saw making decisions to be a natural, normal, and necessary part of life. Paul did receive divine guidance,[3] but he and others also made decisions.[4] Gordon T. Smith writes, "The capacity to make a decision well, to choose wisely and confidently, is a fundamental skill for Christian life and ministry. Few things are so crucial as evidence of spiritual growth and maturity."[5]

God's Promise to Guide

While we are called to make decisions, God also offers assurance that he does guide us. Scripture presents many images of God, including King, Father, Lord, and Shepherd. Each image depicts God as a superior Being who loves us and is in charge of our well-being. After extensive study of the biblical teaching on guidance, M. Blaine Smith says that "I see an overwhelming emphasis in the Bible on a God who *takes the responsibility to guide* us in spite of our confusion over his will." Smith offers these reassuring words:

> Realizing God's concern for me should free me from several common fears. First, I can be free of the fear that *God may not give me the information I need to decide within his will. . . .* Second, I can be released from the fear that *I may not be able to understand God's will if he does convey it to me. . . .* Third, I can be free of the fear *that a past decision made in faith may later be found to be outside of God's will. . . .* Fourth, I can be free of the fear that *my sin may ultimately cause me to miss God's plan for my life.*[6]

When we grasp the depth of God's love and care for us, we can be freed from the fear that despite all our sincere efforts we will somehow miss finding what God wants us to do with our lives. God is fully capable of making his will known to us. He knows each of us as a unique individual and guides us as we uniquely need to be shepherded.

Beth Moore's story illustrates God's creativity and persistence in getting our attention. Moore had been leading an aerobics class for twelve years and had started doing some speaking. She felt God telling her, "I'm calling you out for something different." She resisted, telling him she would quit teaching aerobics when she didn't enjoy it anymore.

One day as she got up to begin teaching, she found her hip was out of joint. "I felt the Holy Spirit say to me, 'Am I going to have to break your leg to get you to listen to me? Let it go!'" She did let go of teaching aerobics, allowing the Lord to give her a platform larger than she could have imagined. Today, she speaks to thousands of women annually and her books have sold millions of copies.[7]

Beth Moore's story illustrates that we do not have to be afraid of missing God's will because God takes the initiative to guide us in our lives when needed. But how might he guide you? What type of guidance can you expect from God as you face important life decisions?

God Still Speaks

God's primary means of guiding us in our decision making is through his Word. Charles Swindoll assures us that "as we derive precepts and principles from the Scriptures, based on a careful, intelligent interpretation of His truth, we're able to apply it in numerous ways to our circumstances today."[8] Studying the Bible molds our thinking so that we are able to see our lives, our world, and ourselves from God's perspective. We partner with God in making decisions whenever we prayerfully make choices in alignment with his revealed will.

God's Word is the most important input we can have in making a decision about our callings. If we ignore or overlook what God says about a particular issue, we deprive ourselves of guidance from the very Source of wisdom: "Unbelievers make sound judgment their first priority in making decisions; believers rely on God's Word. . . . With such a great resource at our disposal, we dare not neglect the counsel of God. Let us not live like those who do not know God."[9]

Guidance for Contemporary Times

How can the Bible be helpful to us in making career decisions and other life calling choices that face us today? After all, we won't find a Bible verse that tells us specifically which college major to choose, if we should change jobs in midlife, whether we should be employed or stay home with our children, or which career option is best for us. In addition, the world of work in biblical times was different from our own. In Jesus' time, for example, most men went into the family business, becoming a merchant, rabbi, carpenter, or shepherd. Most women married early, had children, and took care of their home and family. "What should I do with my life?" was not a burning question of the time.

The biblical world was unlike our own, yet the compass principles revealed in Scripture for making career and life decisions are still relevant for our contemporary lives. As discussed in Chapter Two, life calling compass principle three is that "God calls us to proactive stewardship of our gifts." To apply this biblical principle to making decisions about work and volunteer activities, we need to ask ourselves, *"At this time in my life, how can I best use my gifts, abilities, and other resources to further God's purposes in this world?"* Here are some ways others have expressed this essential stewardship question:

> • God expects you to do work that meets his agenda on earth. It isn't enough to do work that expresses your talents and provides for your needs. You must also ask, *"How does God want to use my life to fulfill his intentions for his world?"* It's critically important that you see that God has given you gifts to advance his kingdom, and not principally to advance your private career (Dick Staub and Jeff Trautman; emphasis added).[10]
>
> • If we are serious about finding God's best for our lives, it doesn't begin with the question, "What do I want and what turns me on?" but *"What does God want and how does God want to use me to make a difference in the world?"* (Tom and Christine Sine; emphasis added).[11]

We live in a complex world and face many difficult decisions not addressed specifically in the Bible. Even so, the Bible plays a critical role in our decision making by showing us what is important to God. The Holy Spirit makes it possible for us to understand God's revealed will and apply it to the specific circumstances of our lives. God can also guide us through the wise counsel of others who help us put biblical principles into practice in the decisions we face. God uses his Word to enlarge the frame in which we see our work and our lives, transforming our perspective from the temporal to the eternal.

Even if we discern no definitive divine guidance, we still can move ahead, trusting that the Holy Spirit is at work within us, enabling us to choose wisely. We partner with God in choosing our callings as we take the initiative to work through a reasoned process of evaluating options in light of biblical principles and our design. With each step, we seek God's guidance in his Word and through prayer, remaining receptive to his instruction should he choose at any point to indicate specifically what he wants us to do.

Guidance Through Circumstances

Many of us find that we have a heightened sensitivity to circumstances when we are facing a big decision. Seeking God's guidance, we may look (or strain) to discern his hand at work in the events happening around us. How are we to interpret events that seem providential? Does God guide us through the circumstances of our lives?

Julie, for example, had been working as a computer programmer for three years. Wanting to use more of her creativity, she thought about getting into Web design. One day she got a call from a friend who had started a business developing Websites for churches and Christian ministries. She needed more help and wanted Julie to join her in the business. Although she could only pay about 75 percent of Julie's current salary, there was the potential of quickly earning more. Hanging up the phone, Julie wondered if this was God's answer to her prayer about which career path to pursue.

Was Julie's job opportunity a sign from God that she should accept the job offer? Or was it simply an opportunity that contained no inherent divine guidance? People sometimes refer to using "open doors" and "closed doors" to discern God's guidance. An opportunity that can be easily pursued could be viewed as an open door, while a situation that lacks opportunity or appears difficult may be seen as a closed door. In seeking guidance for a particular decision, we might tend to interpret an open door as a supernatural sign from God to pursue that path and view a closed door as a divine "no" in regard to a particular choice or direction.

The Bible, however, does not use the term *open door* in connection with praying for guidance in a personal decision; nor does it even mention closed doors. In Scripture, occurrences of the term *open door* refer to opportunities to preach the gospel,[12] not divine signs meant to offer guidance in personal decision making.

Regarding closed doors, Garry Friesen makes this comment: "If [Paul] were sovereignly prevented from pursuing a plan, and yet the plan itself was sound, he simply waited and tried again later. He did not view a blocked endeavor as a 'closed door' sign from God that his plan was faulty. He accepted the fact that he could not pursue the plan at that time. Yet he continued to desire, pray, and plan for the eventual accomplishment of the goal" (see Romans 1:10–13).[13]

John Maxwell counsels that "the road to the next level is always uphill." If we find ourselves coasting downhill in life, making the decisions that take us on the easy route, we risk ending up on the path of least resistance and missing God's best for our lives. An open door may really be a trap door confining us to our comfort zone and keeping us from discovering our true calling. We encounter myriad opportunities, or doors, in our lives. The circumstances of our lives—whether viewed as open or closed doors—must be evaluated carefully in light of God's Word, guidance from the Holy Spirit, our gifts and abilities, wise counsel, and common sense.

The Three Dimensions of Discernment

Discerning our callings requires each of us to find the balance between expecting divine guidance and choosing to make a decision. Our task of discernment has three important dimensions. The first is *maintaining an attitude of expectant openness to God's leading,* seeking to listen not only to what he has already revealed but also to what he is saying to us in the present moment. God's Word is "living and active,"[14] and the Holy Spirit is our Teacher and Counselor.[15]

The second dimension is *taking responsibility to make decisions* about our callings despite uncertainty, difficulty, or fear. Decisions have creative power and are the prelude to action. Making wise decisions is therefore one of the essential skills we need to work on, in partnership with God, to discover and live our callings.

The third essential dimension of discerning our callings may be the most challenging for us: *being willing to do whatever God asks of us.* In making a decision, we must be open to any possibility we think God might be calling us to pursue—even if it requires major changes or action steps we see as being formidable. God calls us to trust him enough to submit *our will* for our lives to *his will* for our lives. God calls us to obedience. He calls us to say "Yes!" to whatever he asks us to do.

The Prayer of Relinquishment

Rick Warren says that "to fulfill your mission will require that you abandon your agenda and accept God's agenda for your life. . . . You stop praying selfish prayers like 'God, bless what I want to do.' Instead you pray, 'God, help me to do what you're blessing!' "[16] Accepting God's agenda for our lives means we are willing to surrender our decisions, goals, hopes, and dreams for our lives if they differ from God's intentions for us.

Veteran filmmaker Ken Wales learned about the miracles that can occur when we are willing to submit our dreams to God's plans. He is the creator of *Christy*, the television drama that aired from 1994 to 1995. Based on the international bestseller by Catherine Marshall, it tells the story of a courageous and spirited young woman who leaves her sheltered city life to teach at a mission school in a remote Appalachian community in 1912. The series made network TV history as viewers saw Christy praying openly to God about the poverty and other struggles of the mountain children who had captured her heart.

In 1975, Wales read *Christy*, which is based on the true experiences of Catherine Marshall's mother, Leonora Wood (the real Christy). He immediately envisioned making a feature film, feeling strongly it was something he had to do. In 1986 he began working on it, but the stock market crash the following year brought an end to the project. In 1990, the president of CBS Television called and offered him the opportunity to produce *Christy* as a prime-time show. Wales told him no; it had to be a feature film first. In 1993, CBS asked again. This time he said yes. Days earlier, he had prayed a prayer of relinquishment, placing his dream of a feature film in God's hands. He had come to understand that by giving up his own dream, something greater could happen. And that is just what occurred. He said that, in hindsight, he could see that "God's timing is perfect. More people saw *Christy* on TV in one night than would have seen the feature film in a lifetime."[17]

Christy ran for twenty-two episodes and experienced moderate success in the ratings. Despite its relatively brief run, it proved to be a real groundbreaker. For the first time in prime-time television, the heroine's actions were portrayed as based on her Christian faith. *Christy* paved the way for the TV series *Touched by an Angel* and *Seventh Heaven*.[18]

Relinquishing our desired direction and goals to God allows him either to give back our dreams with his blessing at the appropriate time or to change us so that the desires of our hearts change as well. When we tightly clutch our dreams, self-image, income level, lifestyle, material possessions, relationships, job title, five-year plan, or familiar surroundings, we are only able to hear our own frightened and rebellious spirit. The quiet promptings of the Holy Spirit may go undetected over our own loud inner voice insisting we know best and must have our own way.

Relinquishing our decisions about our vocational calling means that we release them, giving God possession or control of them. In the act of relinquishment we are again saying, "Not my will, but yours, Father. This is the decision I have made and intend to act on, but I am open to your showing me a different direction. I want to do what *you* want me to do."

We need to be fully committed to making decisions and taking action to implement them, but at the same time we need to acknowledge that God may want to take us down another path. If that is the case, however, it is up to him to show us what it is. Otherwise, we can trust that God will guide our decision making as we seek his will. Then by relinquishing our decisions to God in prayer, we open the door for God to come in and make things happen in his own way for our good and his glory.

Personal Application

1. Dallas Willard says, "It is God's will that we ourselves should have a great part in determining our path through life." Do you think this is true? Why or why not? How does his statement make you feel?

2. What have you been taught in the past about how to find God's will? What have been your beliefs about open doors and closed doors? How have your beliefs had an impact on your decision making?

3. Does this chapter present a perspective on God's will and your role in decision making different from the views you have held? If so, how does this perspective differ?

4. On an emotional level, do you trust that God takes the responsibility to guide you as needed? Why or why not?

8

TOOLBOX OF STRATEGIES FOR MAKING LIFE CALLING DECISIONS

If you don't make up your mind, your unmade mind will unmake you.

E. STANLEY JONES

Decisions have the power to change our lives for the better—or for the worse. Decision making therefore can be difficult when we feel a lot is at stake. Making a decision inescapably means taking a risk. We may fear not succeeding, experiencing disapproval from family or friends, or being ultimately disappointed by our choice.

In addition, many of us have never been taught specifically how to make decisions, especially when it comes to making decisions about our callings. If we are not sure what criteria to use in choosing a career, for example, we may look primarily at objective factors such as salary and benefits, or ultimately make a decision based on our intuition or feelings about our choices. We may know there are other things we should consider but not be sure exactly what they are.

Given the challenges of decision making, it is understandable why some people avoid it. Instead of making choices, they tend to let their path through life be shaped by outside circumstances and decisions others make for them. They may say "I fell into my career" or "I just found myself in this situation," which conveys a sense of letting life happen instead of intentionally choosing a direction.

Strategies for Making Wise Decisions

Accepting responsibility to be a good steward of our gifts means that we also must accept responsibility for making decisions. This chapter contains four decision-making strategies to help you compare your design and other important factors in your life with the options you have identified as potential career paths or volunteer activities. They guide you in thinking through the practical aspects of your decision and enable you to examine the spiritual dimensions as well. Your Life Calling Map serves as a helpful tool as you use these strategies for making decisions about your work and other important life roles.

Strategy One: Comparing Options with Your Design

This strategy allows you to compare each of your career or volunteer ministry/service possibilities with your core work values, transferable skills, and compelling interests. The results enable you to see more clearly how these alternatives fit the dimensions of your unique design. This exercise can help you be a wise steward, or manager, of your God-given gifts and abilities.

1. On the Options Comparison Grid (Table 8.2), list the three or four career or volunteer options of most interest. (You can also include your current or most recent job for comparison, if you like.)

2. Fill in your top five core work values from your Life Calling Map, your top five transferable skills, and your top five compelling interests.

3. Determine the degree of importance, or the "weight" (WT), of each item by dividing *twenty-five points* among the items on each grid. *The more important the item to you, the more points you give it.* (See the sample portion of the options comparison grid in Table 8.1.) Though not statistically grounded, dividing twenty-five points does allow you to express your evaluation of the relative importance of the five items.

4. Respond to the question, "How likely is each option to meet this value or use this skill/interest?" (3 = very likely, 2 = somewhat likely, 1 = unlikely). Record the appropriate number in each box on the grid.

5. Multiply that number (representing the likelihood) times the weight of the item, as in Table 8.1, and write the result in the appropriate box.

6. Total your responses.

7. After completing all three parts of the grid, add up the totals for the career or volunteer options to determine a cumulative total for each.

TABLE 8.1. SAMPLE OPTIONS COMPARISON GRID.

(1) Core work values	Weight	Career or Volunteer Options			
		Manager in a Nonprofit Organization	Buy/Run "ABC" Franchise	Certified Financial Planner	Bank Manager (Current Job)
Independence	9	2 x 9 = 18	3 x 9 = 27	2 x 9 = 18	1 x 9 = 9
Creativity/Innovation	5	2 x 5 = 10	3 x 5 = 15	2 x 5 = 10	1 x 5 = 5
Help others	5	2 x 5 = 10	3 x 5 = 15	3 x 5 = 15	2 x 5 = 10
Balance	4	3 x 4 = 12	1 x 4 = 4	2 x 4 = 8	2 x 4 = 8
Power/Authority	2	2 x 2 = 4	3 x 2 = 6	2 x 2 = 4	2 x 2 = 4
(1) Totals		= 54	= 67	= 55	= 36

TABLE 8.2. OPTIONS COMPARISON GRID.

(1) Core work values	Weight	Career or Volunteer Options			
(1) Totals					

TABLE 8.2. OPTIONS COMPARISON GRID, *continued*

Career or Volunteer Options

(2) Transferable skills	Weight				
(2) Totals					
(3) Compelling interests	Weight				
(3) Totals					
Grand totals (1, 2, and 3)					

Interpreting Your Results

As you look at your grand totals, you may find that one particular option scored significantly higher (more than ten points higher) than the others did. If so, the next three decision-making strategies will help you evaluate further if this indeed is the best option for your calling within work or a volunteer role.

You may also find that ten or fewer points separate some of your top-scoring options, indicating that these alternatives are relatively equal in using these dimensions of your design. The following strategies can help you assess further which option is the best choice.

Strategy Two: Assessing Pros and Cons

Writing down pros and cons for a particular decision enables us to identify what our most important criteria really are so that we can rationally evaluate them. If we try to process information about a decision in our head (as opposed to writing it down) we are prone to being swayed by emotionally charged factors such as the salary and perceived security of a job, and we may discount or miss some other significant factors altogether.

In addition, this strategy is designed to help you consider the advantages and disadvantages of each career or volunteer option from two time perspectives: the near future and the more distant future. We are often tempted to make decisions on the basis of the short-term pluses and minuses. When making a decision about our callings, however, we must also consider how they will affect our lives, and the lives of others, in the long run. Considering only the short-term impact of a decision can lead us to choose an option that is convenient but may not be God's best for us.

1. Note the Pros and Cons Grid (Table 8.3). In your journal or notebook, make a similar grid to evaluate each option you are considering.

2. Define for yourself the time periods short-term and long-term. (For example, for one person short-term might be four months and for another person it might be when they finish a degree in two years.)

3. Use your Life Calling Map and the research you have done on the options to list the pros and cons for each. Place an asterisk by any factors that are particularly important to you. (See Table 8.4 for an example.)

TABLE 8.3. THE PROS AND CONS GRID.

Option:

	Pros	Cons
Short-term (time period = _____)		
Long-term (time period = _____)		

TABLE 8.4. SAMPLE PROS AND CONS GRID.

Option: Manager in a nonprofit organization

	Pros	Cons
Short-term (time period = next 6 months)	• More similar to past experience than other options* • Salaried position • Easiest transition • There are many nonprofits I would be excited to work for	• May not be different enough from what I'm currently doing • May have to move* • Limited independence • May entail pay cut
Long-term (time period = next fifteen years)	• Could lead to opportunity to run a nonprofit • Opportunity to build relationships with other nonprofit leaders • Opportunity to make a difference*	• May feel creativity is stifled • May not have enough growth opportunities

Interpreting Your Results

Here are some things to consider as you review this exercise:

• Look at your lists of pros and cons. Do the factors represent not only what you want to *get* from a position but also what the position allows you to *give*? We are called to be good stewards of our God-given gifts in order to make a difference in the world.

• Is your evaluation of any of your cons affected by fear? For example, do you view some possibilities negatively because you think they will not pay enough, or will be challenging to get into, or will require you to move outside of your comfort zone? Prayerfully consider what God would have you do. Our fears can get in the way of living our callings.

• You may have an option that appears to be the best choice overall, but it requires additional education, training, or experience before you can transition into it. If you want to make a more immediate change in your work, consider making a two-part transition. Your next transition would be to something that fits you better than your current position, is obtainable in the near future, and allows you time and opportunity to gain the credentials or experience needed for your longer-range transition. This may be a time in which God is calling you to prepare yourself for a future role in which you can make a significant contribution.

After reviewing the pros and cons for each option, which appears to be the best choice? Why?

Strategy Three: Evaluating Career Options in Light of Biblical Principles

The third strategy gives you an opportunity to apply the life calling compass principles (keeping your primary calling primary, using your gifts to meet needs in the world, and being a proactive steward of your gifts) to career and volunteer options you are considering. We partner with God in decision making as we look at our life and our career from the viewpoint of his revealed will.

1. List the career or volunteer options of most interest in the top row of Table 8.5. (When evaluating volunteer positions, you can omit responding to the principles related to money.) You may also want to list your current or most recent job for comparison.

2. Rate each option in each category on a 1–5 scale (1 = very little opportunity to do this; 5 = great opportunity to do this).

3. Add up the total points for each option.

TABLE 8.5. EVALUATING OPTIONS IN LIGHT OF BIBLICAL PRINCIPLES.

How Well Will Each Career or Volunteer Option Enable Me to:	Option 1:	Option 2:	Option 3:	Option 4:
Use my gifts in the service of others? (1 Peter 4:10)				
Use skills, abilities, interests, and so on that I enjoy? (Ecclesiastes 3:13)				
Provide for my physical and material needs (and those of my family)? (1 Timothy 5:8; 2 Thessalonians 3:10) *Note:* Take care to distinguish between "needs" and "wants."				
Meet my family's spiritual and emotional needs? (Deuteronomy 6:6–7; Ephesians 6:4; 1 Timothy 3:4–5) (How much time, for example, will each option allow me to devote to my spouse and family? How much emotional energy will each option leave for them?)				
Earn enough to be able to contribute to the needs of others? (Ephesians 4:28)				

TABLE 8.5. EVALUATING OPTIONS
IN LIGHT OF BIBLICAL PRINCIPLES, *continued*.

How Well Will Each Career or Volunteer Option Enable Me to:	Option 1:	Option 2:	Option 3:	Option 4:
Make progress in developing Christlike attitudes and actions? (Galatians 5:22–23)				
Avoid becoming greedy, proud, lustful, dishonest, arrogant, envious, deceitful, manipulative, or otherwise tempted to sin? (Colossians 3:5–10; 1 Timothy 6:10–11)				
Maintain my honesty and integrity, act in a moral and ethical manner, and be "salt" and "light" in the workplace? (Matthew 5:13–16)				
Demonstrate an attitude of service to others? (Matthew 20:28; Mark 9:35)				
Allow me to participate in the work of God's kingdom? (1 Corinthians 15:58; Matthew 28:19–20; 1 Corinthians 3:8–9)				
Allow me sufficient time for my other secondary callings, such as being involved in my church?				
Other principles I would like to add:				
Total points for each option:				

Interpreting Your Results

Place an asterisk by each principle that you feel is particularly important for you to consider in making your decision. What is significant about each for you?

_____

_____

_____

_____

You may find that the point totals for your options are similar. Are there any options, however, that you find are not in alignment with God's revealed will? If so, how?

_____

_____

_____

_____

Strategy Four: Defending Your Decision

In this exercise, you will develop a defense for each of your career or volunteer options. In this mental role play you create a defense for each, seeking to persuade someone who is not convinced it is a wise choice. This strategy helps you in critically examining your possible alternatives.

1. Think of a person, real or imaginary, who does not believe that a specific option is a good choice for you.
2. In your journal or notebook, respond to these items for *each* career or volunteer option of interest:
   a. Name the career or volunteer option you are defending.
   b. Describe why the other person does not support this choice.
   c. Defend this option by listing the reasons it is the best choice for you (and your family) at this point in your life. (Include a description of how it allows you to be a good steward of your gifts, abilities, and other resources.)

    d. Explain why you believe God could be calling you to pursue this option.

    e. Other comments?

Interpreting Your Results

Review your defense for each option. From this exercise, which option seems to be the best choice? Why?

_____

_____

_____

_____

_____

Review your responses for each of the four exercises. Which option appears to be the best choice overall? Why?

_____

_____

_____

_____

_____

The Value of Feedback in Making Your Decision

At this point you may have identified the option you think is the best choice for your callings within work or other life roles, or you may still feel uncertain as to the choice you should make. Regardless of which category you are in, we recommend you talk over the option you are considering with at least two people who will give you honest and beneficial feedback. (Your Live Your Calling partner or group provides some ready counselors with whom to talk through your decision.) Each of us has only a subjective view of our situation and ourselves and therefore can benefit greatly from the more objective viewpoints other people can offer.

Feedback from others can also help you counter those tendencies of your personality type that may lead you astray in decision making. For example, people who are "judging" (*J* in the personality type inventory of Assessment Four in Chapter Three) like to get things decided. Since they usually dislike having things open-ended, making a decision gives a sense of relief. The tendency of *J* types is therefore to make a decision too quickly without examining enough possible choices or gathering sufficient information about them. *J* types may benefit from others holding them accountable for not making a decision prematurely.

On the other hand, "perceiving" types (*P* in the personality type inventory) usually like keeping their options open. They may enjoy gathering information about possible choices yet resist making a decision for fear of boxing themselves in and compromising their ability to find just the right option. Or they may tend to make rather impulsive decisions without adequate information. *P* types may benefit from having someone hold them accountable for making a well-thought-through decision by a particular date. Otherwise, they may find that their lives are being shaped more by random circumstances than responsible decisions.

Feedback from people we trust can help us examine our alternatives from several perspectives, clarify the relative merit of each, and confirm the decision we favor. If you still feel confused after completing these decision-making strategies, you might consider finding a counselor who is experienced in helping people with career and life planning from a Christian perspective. A gifted counselor can help you process information effectively or work through any issues that may be impeding your ability to make a decision. Overall, wise counsel from others can increase your confidence that you are making the best decisions about your callings within work and volunteer roles.

Feeling Terminally Stuck

Although feeling a level of uncertainty when faced with a decision is normal, some people experience more extreme reactions at such times. They may feel hopelessly stuck and not know what to do. There is a difference between being *undecided* and being *indecisive*. People who are *undecided* are capable of making a decision; they have just not yet gathered enough information or evaluated their choices thoroughly enough. Those who are *indecisive*, in contrast, have personal issues that interfere with their ability to make decisions.

People who are chronically indecisive typically experience a high level of anxiety when faced with a decision. If you find yourself to be extremely anxious, confused, overwhelmed, or exhibiting avoidance behavior (such as having many excuses for not making a decision), consider seeking help from a qualified professional to uncover the reasons for your indecisiveness. Indecisiveness affects all areas of life; dealing with it head-on in the career area can free a person to move forward in other areas of life as well. Getting stuck can signal that some part of us needs healing. God is ready, willing, and able to help us find the wholeness we need to discover and live our calling.

Finding Peace with Your Decisions

Many of us experience at least some degree of uncertainty after making an important decision. Uneasiness can occur for a variety of reasons. Sometimes it is a sign that we have overlooked one or more important factors while identifying possibilities or making our decision. Someone may also feel unsettled because he or she has not had much experience making intentional decisions and committing to a new direction. It takes time and practice to get comfortable with new skills and ways of thinking.

Most of us experience some doubt, however, because a decision usually entails elements of the unknown and some degree of risk. Typically, there is no choice that has only overwhelming advantages and no drawbacks. Nor can we always anticipate all the ways in which a decision will affect our lives. Even when we believe we are responding to God's leading, we can still feel uncertain.

Sometimes people think they have made the wrong decision if they don't feel a sense of peace about it. Examining our feelings carefully is important so they do not lead us astray. For example, John initially attributed a lack of peace to God telling him he should not pursue the career path he had chosen. When he honestly examined his feelings, however, he admitted that the feeling really was anxiety about doing something new and having to move out of his comfort zone. Our feelings give us important information, but we need to interpret them with care so they do not hinder us from living our calling.

Practicing good decision-making skills gives us increased confidence in making important life decisions. We grow in maturity as we strengthen our ability to think logically, plan strategically, and apply biblical wisdom to our everyday lives. These capabilities equip us to be more fully used by God in the world. As we use sound decision-making strategies *and* seek God's guidance through his Word, prayer, the Holy Spirit, and wise counsel, we position ourselves to partner effectively with him in discerning and living our callings.

Personal Application

1. Think of an important decision that you faced in the past. How did you go about making the decision? In retrospect, is there anything you would change about how you made it? If so, what? Why?
2. Carry out the decision-making strategies in this chapter that will help you accomplish your goals for using this book:

   If you want to identify career options, we recommend you complete all four strategies.

   If you want to identify volunteer ministry/service options, choose one or more strategies that seem helpful to you.
3. Once you have completed the exploration and decision-making strategies, identify the career or volunteer option(s) that fit you best and represent what you believe God is calling you to pursue.
4. If desired, write out a prayer relinquishing to God any career or volunteer choice you have decided to pursue.

PART FIVE

TRANSFORMING VISION INTO ACTION

9

PLANNING YOUR JOURNEY

It isn't what you wish to do, it's what you will do for God that transforms your life.

HENRIETTA MEARS

Kevin Franklin, a writer for a local paper, intended to climb Tam O'Shanter Peak in the mountains north of Tucson, Arizona. He admitted that he had never quite gotten around to getting the appropriate maps. Standing in the center of a large basin looking at a number of peaks in the distance, he discovered that the large-scale map he had brought didn't pinpoint which peak was his desired destination; nor did it give details of the terrain surrounding him. Nevertheless, he set out toward the peak he determined looked most like a tam-o'-shanter, the Scottish beret with a pom-pom.

After hiking for a while, he knew where he had come from and how to get back, but wasn't sure where he was. Some, he said, might even have said he was lost. He preferred thinking of it as "losing contact with his map." After roving for a while, he finally found the beretlike peak, made his climb, and headed back to town.

Once home, he examined the maps he should have taken with him and realized he had climbed the wrong peak. He had ascended an unnamed peak some three miles southeast of the Tam O'Shanter. Deciding that this had been an adventure rather than a mistake, he wrote,

"Any fool can get to a specific geographic location given enough maps.
. . . The challenge today is to end up someplace other than you intended.
It's the art of indeterminate wandering."[1]

Navigating Through Life

Serendipitous adventures encountered on unmapped trails can be fun
for a day hike, but few of us want to spend our lives in "indeterminate
wandering." There are many people who just meander through life, and
then there are those who are traveling toward an intentional destination.
This chapter further equips you not only to discern your destination but
also to plan the best route for getting there successfully.

Each of us is the navigator in life's journey. The compass principles
(keeping our primary calling primary, using our gifts to meet needs in
the world, and being proactive stewards of our gifts) orient us to the true
north of eternal guidelines for achieving a significant life. Jesus cautioned
us that our natural human preoccupation with the worries of life and
the desire for wealth and other things[2] can get us off course and make
our lives ineffective. The compass principles hone our sense of direction so that we don't lose our way amid the challenges and tempta-
tions of this world.

We each are given the task of finding our way through the wilder-
ness territories of life. You have been developing your Life Calling Map,
which thus far represents key dimensions of your God-given design. It
has guided you in exploring and making decisions about your vocational
calling. You are now moving beyond mapping your design to planning
your journey by adding three additional dimensions to your Life Calling Map. They create a framework for looking at the whole of your life
and a context for understanding more fully how you are called to use
your design.

In this chapter, we introduce *personal mission statements*, which are vivid
pictures or descriptions of your desired destination in life; *priority goals*,
which serve as progress markers on your life course; and *action plans*, which
outline the route you take to reach your goals. (In the next chapter you

are guided through developing each of these components of your Life Calling Map.)

As you develop mission statements, goals, and action plans, you are not taking control of your life away from God. Rather, you are doing your part to fulfill your life's mission by making plans to take the necessary actions to accomplish the things you are called to do. One meaning of destination is *the ultimate purpose for which something is created or intended.* By pointing you in the right direction and keeping you on course along the way, your Life Calling Map helps ensure that the destination you reach in your life is the one that both you and God intended.

Personal Mission Statements

Personal mission statements are word pictures, or descriptions, of your God-sized visions for your life. In the next chapter, you have the opportunity to write a mission statement for your primary calling, and for each of your most significant secondary callings (life roles) and record them on your Life Calling Map. Effective organizations create mission statements to articulate and keep them on track with their primary purpose. An organizational mission statement describes why the company exists and what it intends to accomplish. Your personal mission statements describe what you believe God is calling you to do and your sense of purpose in living your calling within each key life role. Viewed together, your mission statements create a composite picture of the life you want to live.

Mission Statements Help You Get What You Really Want in Life

One of Stephen Covey's seven habits of highly effective people is to begin with the end in mind.[3] Writing your mission statements does just that by requiring you to think through what you are aiming for in each of your callings. Our lives are often so busy that we just "do," going about our daily activities without thinking what we really want to achieve in our lives. Your mission statements enable you to identify what you believe God is calling you to accomplish in each of your significant life roles so you can avoid in-determinate wandering.

Developing a personal mission statement for each of your signifi-cant life roles benefits you in several ways. Your mission statements *bring more balance and wholeness to your life.* Acknowledging in writing that your life consists of several important roles helps prevent getting so absorbed in carrying out one role (such as your work) that you neglect other roles that are equally as important—or even more important—to your over-all life calling.

Your mission statements help you *select and prioritize the activities in your life.* They assist you in organizing your days, weeks, and years to ac-complish what really matters to you. More important, they empower you to accomplish the things that really matter to God. Each of us is given the same twenty-four hours in the day, yet some people achieve much more with their time.

Mission Statements Focus Your Energy

Many people "leak" energy in a lot of directions. Lacking direction and purpose, their days are spent doing work they don't really like and pass-ing time by watching TV, surfing the Internet, and doing other things that aren't really satisfying. As someone once said, in the absence of a clear purpose "we become strangely loyal to performing trivia."

Those without direction may also find themselves dabbling in many things, yet not really excelling in any of them. Like an incandescent light bulb, their time and energy is expended in many directions. *Where did all the time go?* they may wonder as they watch the years pass, find their dis-contentment and discouragement deepening, and recognize that their lives are going nowhere.

In contrast to the diffused energy of a light bulb, your mission state-ments enable you to focus your energy like a laser beam. The concen-trated energy of a laser is so powerful that it can cut through several inches of solid steel. Mission statements direct your energy, giving you a way of taking your God-given gifts plus your sense of vision and "aim-ing them both in a precise direction."[4] Your personal mission statements furnish clarity of direction and empower you to say yes to the things that should be a part of your life, and no to those things that lead you away from your mission in life.

Compelling personal mission statements *motivate you to take risks* as well. Taking a risk means doing something without being guaranteed a positive outcome. Risks are an inherent part of living a life of significance. Without a doubt, they are a part of living the life to which God calls you. Personal mission statements enable you to look at the big picture of your life within the context of eternity, and better understand that risks are often the essential means to an end.

Priority Goals

Your personal mission statements express your understanding of the callings God has given you in your life. The act of defining your callings by writing your mission statements changes your thinking and focuses your vision for your life. However, they are not magical statements that will become reality just by putting them in writing and displaying them on your desk or the refrigerator. Living your calling requires you to develop an intentional plan to move you from where you are today to where you believe God is calling you to be. Identifying your *priority goals* is the next key step for incorporating your mission statements into your day-to-day life.

A goal is a clear, specific objective. Goals personalize and particularize your mission statements. Setting goals is the catalyst for bringing your God-inspired visions to life. Your vision of your callings must be translated into specific actions; otherwise they remain a distant summons instead of becoming your life's experience. Stephen Covey alerts us to the need to define explicit actions and not just focus on the big picture: "If we don't translate vision into action, we lose touch with reality, become idealistic dreamers, and lose credibility with ourselves and with others."[5]

Goals focus our attention. Clear objectives flip a switch within us, unleashing the energy and power to transform vision into reality. Zig

Ziglar stresses the importance of goals with this pithy fact of life: "You will never realize more than a small fraction of your potential as a wandering generality. You must become a meaningful specific."[6] Developing goals and a plan for achieving them enables you to participate with God to "become a meaningful specific" in his great plan. Your priority goals serve as progress markers for determining where you are and assessing how well you are doing on your journey of living your calling.

Goals Activate Your "Selective Perception"

God has made us to be goal-pursuing beings. He has created our minds to move toward our goals even when we are not consciously thinking about them. We humans have been created with "selective perception," meaning that our minds automatically extract information from our environment that pertains to our goals.

Advertisers, for example, spend lots of time and money bombarding us with ads for their products and services. Although we encounter numerous ads each day, typically we only focus on those that feature products of interest to us. If you need a new watch, car tires, or shoes, your selective perception goes to work, causing ads for those items to jump out at you.

Similarly, for years we advertised our career services on Christian radio, yet we would have people who regularly listened to the station say they had heard our ad "for the first time." Often, hearing our ad coincided with their newfound desire to find a different type of work. Their minds tuned in to the radio ad because it related to their desire to change jobs. The clearer you are about your goals, therefore, the more your mind automatically goes to work pointing you to information and resources that help you meet your goals.

Goals Elevate You to the Top 3 Percent

Many people just let life happen to them. You, however, join a small, elite group of people who have chosen to live intentional lives when you develop and write down your priority goals. Ziglar said, "Everyone has individual goals that might be positive or negative, but 97 percent of the people in our society do not have an organized goals program. . . . Only 3 percent of all Americans have goals programs designed to reap the most benefits from life itself."[7] Completing the exercises in the next chapter sets you apart from 97 percent of other Americans and positions you to experience the life God intends for you to live.

Even a simple goals program enables you to do more than you ever thought possible in your life. You will be repaid many times over for the effort you expend in developing your goals program. "Writing down goals . . . may sound like a lot of work," acknowledges Tim Hansel. "But when they are tied up with your vision, your dreams, about the things you love to do and want to do," he continues, "they easily become part of the path to your dream. And they never seem like work again. If you don't set your own goals, you will always be accepting other people's goals."[8] Living your calling requires focusing on what you believe God wants you to do with the hours, days, and years of your life, and identifying the goals he calls you to achieve.

Plan for Action

Your *action plan* is a tool for translating your mission statements into priority goals and action steps. It is a tool for making the accomplishment of your goals achievable. Many people have goals, dreams, or visions to which they feel God is calling them. They may fail to take action, however, because the dream or vision seems so large, distant, or overwhelming that they don't even know where to begin. They give up on the dream before they even get started. Your action plan can transform the seemingly impossible into the actually achievable.

Your action plan breaks down your God-sized callings into bite-sized pieces by outlining and organizing the chronological action steps needed to accomplish your goals. Your action plan makes a crucial difference in your life, moving you from daydreaming about what God has gifted and called you to do to making it happen. If you consistently take small steps in the right direction, you will arrive at significant destinations.

The Illusion of "Magical Thinking"

"Magical thinking" is anticipating that our lives will change without having to take sustained action. Most of us have dabbled in magical thinking at one time or another. Have any thoughts like these ever crossed your mind?

> "If I read this book on (financial management, weight loss, career change, prayer), it will change my life."
>
> "If I sign up for the health club membership, I'll finally be slim and physically fit!"
>
> "If I win the lottery, I'll be able to have the life I really want!"

We nurture a hope that some day some set of circumstances will somehow sweep into our lives from somewhere (you can see that thoughts of this sort are rather vague) and transform our lives—without our having to take any risks or exert ourselves to take action. If a person wants to lose weight, however, he has to do more than just dream about being slim. If an individual is in debt and her financial situation is a mess, she has to do more than just worry about the negative balance in her checking account. If we want to know our vocational calling, we need to do more than just pray about it; we also need to seek it. Without taking the right actions there will be no real change in our lives.

The Power of Disciplined Action

Living your calling requires combining prayer with action. You are God's fellow worker, his partner in doing his work in this world. Work requires action. Don't fall into the trap of just waiting and praying for God to make something happen in your life. Ted Engstrom, president emeritus of World Vision, writes in *Pursuit of Excellence:* "Perhaps part of our problem is just some defective theology. Many of us have difficulty living with the biblical truth that a sovereign God is doing it all and the parallel truth that man has not only been given complete responsibility for his actions but is commanded to take action. This is part of the tension between theology and living, a tension that will never be nor should it be resolved."[9]

Prayer is an essential part of living our primary calling and each of our secondary callings. Walt Kallestad writes that "praying about your dreams transfers the dream to God, transforms you, and transcends your limitations."[10] Prayer connects you with the Source of wisdom and power, keeps you focused on what is truly important in life, opens doors, and prepares the way for action. Prayer is the prelude to and companion of action. God also calls us, however, to take action. The Bible is clear that "faith by itself, if it is not accompanied by action, is dead."[11]

We can err on either side. We can feel that everything depends on us, which leads to becoming driven people who are not listening for God's call. Or we can wait and pray for God to put us (somehow) exactly where he wants us to be. The latter leads to passivity; stagnation in the growth of skill, wisdom, and maturity; and missing opportunities that God has prepared for us.

We must pray and seek God's guidance. We must also plan and take action. You are the only person on earth who can use your God-given gifts and talents to live your God-sized callings. Without action, your gifts go undeveloped and unused, and your calling remains unfulfilled. Disciplined action is the bridge between dreaming about your calling and living the life to which God calls you.

Sharpening Your Sense of Direction

When finding their way in unfamiliar territory, some people instinctively know where to go; others wander around without a clue. The difference lies in an internal sense of direction. Researcher R. Robin Baker believes that we are all born with an innate sense of direction and then either develop it as we get older or lose it from lack of use.

The good news is that even for those who frequently feel befuddled in finding their way, their sense of direction can be "resurrected and trained." The strategies Baker suggests for refining our ability to navigate successfully include learning where north is in relation to our surroundings, studying the maps of the area to get the lay of the land in our mind, and resisting the urge to charge down the path before orienting ourselves as to where we are and where we want to go.[12]

The compass principles and your Life Calling Map sharpen your sense of direction for navigating through life. Developing your personal mission statements, priority goals, and action plan adds immensely to the value and usefulness of your Life Calling Map. They help you stay on course; avoid unnecessary detours and wasted time; and infuse your life with the energy that comes from experiencing momentum, anticipation, and satisfying accomplishment. As you complete your action steps and accomplish your priority goals, you will fulfill your God-given dreams instead of just being a dreamer.

Personal Application

1. What do you see as being most beneficial about developing personal mission statements?
2. What is your reaction to writing down your goals? If your initial response is less than positive, how might you benefit from doing this?
3. Can you think of a time when you engaged in magical thinking? What was the result?

10

TOOLBOX OF STRATEGIES
FOR LIVING YOUR CALLING

---

*Do not ask the Lord to guide your footsteps if you are not willing
to move your feet.*   AUTHOR UNKNOWN

Oswald Chambers wrote, "Dreaming about a thing in order to do
it properly is right; but dreaming about it when we should be
doing it is wrong."[1] Being a proactive steward of our gifts means we
have to move from dreaming to doing. Even a calling received on a
mountaintop must be lived in the valley. Living your divine callings
requires getting to work and figuring out how to bring them to life in
your everyday world.

Translating a Calling into an Action Plan

After working with thousands of people, we know how difficult transitions can be, particularly when someone has been in his or her occupation for many years. We have tremendous respect for our clients who
follow through in making career transitions, especially when doing so
means they have to face such challenges as financial risk, perceived loss
of status, and walking into the unknown in order to do the work they
believe God has created them to do.

Jerod had a lot invested in his career. He earned a graduate degree in planetary science from a prestigious institution and worked for NASA for five years. Although it was difficult for him to picture walking away from his career, he felt strongly that there was something else that would better use his gifts. After investing a lot of time in exploring career options, praying, and soul searching, he decided to pursue becoming a high school science teacher with a secondary goal of coaching sports.

"I feel like I have more to offer as a teacher than as an engineer," he explained. "The opportunity to teach, encourage kids, and be a positive influence on their lives is more important to me than the perceived glamour of working on high-profile space projects. Teaching would allow me to better use my giftedness in dealing with people than being an engineer does. I can think of no greater calling or more valuable use of my life than to dedicate it to working with kids."

Having made this courageous decision, he and his wife, Laura, had to figure out how to turn their dream into reality so he could begin living his vocational calling. His career change was all the more challenging because they wanted to relocate halfway across the country, and there was no second income to live on during the transition. Laura was at home with their toddler and expecting another child.

Writing his personal mission statements, which expressed his sense of purpose and calling in his future career, generated the motivation for change. Developing priority goals outlined the progress markers for his transition. Creating an action plan laid out the route for change. Jerod developed and implemented his action plan, which God then added to and redirected in surprising ways. Jerod and Laura's lives are living examples of how God does step in when we step out in faith.

When Jerod spoke to his boss about quitting his job at NASA and his upcoming move, he was unexpectedly offered the opportunity to be a full-time telecommuter for a year. NASA outfitted his new home with a computer and the software he needed to do his job from home, two thousand miles away from his former workplace. They also gave him a raise! This unanticipated offer kept Jerod from having to work several part-time jobs to support his family while he attended school to get his teaching certificate. His boss later extended his telecommuting job another year while he completed his course work and then agreed to keep him on as a part-time consultant during the summers.

During his job hunt, Jerod turned down three job offers over a period of a few months because none of them was the right fit. Weeks later, Laura found an online job listing for a position in a high school Jerod hadn't even considered as a possibility. He applied, was interviewed, and a week later was offered the position.

Jerod and Laura have taken a lot of risks and made many sacrifices for Jerod to pursue his vocational calling. The risks, however, have paid off. Both the principal and Jerod receive phone calls from parents who express what a great teacher he is. The students gravitate toward him, eager to talk outside of class. They are very impressed that he would leave NASA to come be their teacher.

Laura commented on her amazement at how easily he has taken to the role of being a teacher: "It's like he was born to do this job." Jerod is very glad he made this huge change in his life. He says he has received so many confirmations along the way that he and Laura have no doubt this is what God has planned for him for this time in his life.

"It hasn't always been easy on me or my family," Jerod said, "and the steps we've taken haven't always been what we originally planned to do, but they were all a part of God's perfect plan for us. The best part is I'm using the gifts God gave to me. I feel more fulfilled than I ever did working for NASA. I'm tired from all the planning, paper grading, and getting up a lot earlier than I used to, but I absolutely love what I do."

Action Strategies for Living Your Calling

The three strategies given here describe how you can translate your callings into action steps. As you develop your personal mission statements, priority goals, and action plans for living your calling, you are completing the remaining portions of your Life Calling Map.

Strategy One: Developing Personal Mission Statements

Your Life Calling Map has spaces for you to record your personal mission statement for your primary calling and for four of your most important secondary callings, or life roles. You are not seeking to write perfect statements; you are simply describing your understanding of what God is calling you to do in your life right now. You may find that your mission statements need to be modified in the future; they most likely will grow and change as your understanding of your callings grows and changes.

Schedule your own mini-retreat to craft your personal mission statements. A mini-retreat can be as simple as going to a park, library, or other place where you won't be distracted and can focus on what God is calling you to do in your life. Carve out some time, whether it is a weekend away or a few mornings while the kids are at school, to complete this important focusing activity and spiritual exercise.

Mission Statement for Your Primary Calling. We suggest that you choose a Bible verse to write on your Life Calling Map that expresses your understanding of your primary calling. (For example, see verses such as Psalm 23:1; Matthew 6:33; Micah 6:8; and Matthew 22:37–39.) Next, draft a personal mission statement that describes what your primary calling means to you. (See Chapter One for a description of your primary calling.) After discussing it with your Live Your Calling Group, finalize your mission statement and write it on your map. Here are two examples:

- My mission is to love God with all my heart, soul, and mind, and to show his love to others, including sharing the good news of salvation and new life in Christ.
- My mission is to be a good steward of my gifts, and to honor and please God in all that I do in my life.

Mission Statements for Your Secondary Callings. Identify the four most important secondary callings in your life right now (life roles such as worker, student, son, daughter, spouse, parent, church member, specific church role—elder, deacon, Sunday school teacher, member of specific organization, citizen, friend, neighbor). Jot them down (in your journal or on another sheet of paper) and rank-order them in terms of their importance to you in your life.

Reflect on what you believe God is calling you to in each role. What do you long to accomplish in each role with God's power? What is your God-sized vision for your calling in each role? You may also want to ask yourself, "If Jesus were writing these mission statements with me, what would he want me to include in them?"

Wherever appropriate, include relevant information about your God-given design. Look at your Life Calling Map, especially the sections on transferable skills, spiritual gifts, and compelling interests. Then think about your purpose in using these skills, gifts, and interests, the need(s) that you are passionate about serving, and your sense of calling in this role. A sample format you can use is this: "My mission is to use my skills of _____, _____, and _____, and my interest in _____ to (or for the purpose of) _____." (See the examples that follow.)

Once you are satisfied with your personal mission statements, record them on your Life Calling Map. You will notice that on your map the mission statements for your secondary callings are recorded under your mission statement for your primary calling. This arrangement visually illustrates that your secondary callings flow out of, and are subordinate to, your primary calling.

Here are examples of personal mission statements for secondary callings (life roles):

Life Role: Worker (You can put a job title here, if you desire.)

• My mission is to use my skills in teaching, organizing, and interpersonal communication, along with my knowledge of math and science, to help students better understand themselves and the universe in which we live.

• My mission is to use my skills of drawing, storytelling, and humor to create visual illustrations that encourage, inform, and entertain people for the purpose of inspiring them to use their lives fully for God.

• My mission is to combine my skills of evaluation, working with financial data, and organizing with my interests in business and economics to invest individuals' and organizations' money and help them accomplish their God-given purposes more effectively.

• My mission is to use my skills of designing, planning, and providing hospitality and my knowledge of business and agriculture to create a working farm and retreat center that promotes the physical, emotional, and spiritual health of its guests.

• My mission is to use my skills in remodeling buildings and my interest in the needs of the elderly to rehab their homes, making their daily lives easier and enabling them to be self-sufficient as long as possible.

Life Role: Church Member (that is, a regular participant in a local church body)

• My mission as a member of New Life Community Church is to worship God; grow into Christian maturity; use my gifts of teaching and encouragement to help others in my church grow in their faith; and bring others to know Jesus and become involved in the life of this church.

• (You can also write a mission statement for a particular ministry you have in your church.) My mission in running the sound board is to use my technical skills and musical knowledge to help ensure that the pastor's message and the worship music are presented as effectively as possible.

• My mission as a kitchen volunteer is to use my skills in organizing and cooking, my gift of hospitality, and my experience of cooking for large groups to make people feel welcomed and loved.

Life Role: Spouse

• My mission as a husband is to love and serve my wife; to help her become the person God created her to be; to head this family responsibly and lovingly according to biblical principles; and to the best of my ability, to provide physical and spiritual protection for my wife and children.

• My mission as a wife is to demonstrate to my husband through my words and actions that he is loved, appreciated, and respected; to support his becoming the person God wants him to be; and to be his partner in creating our marriage and family into what God desires for them to be.

Life Role: Parent

• My mission as a father is to provide leadership; to help my children know Jesus as their Lord and Savior, and grow in their Christian faith; to give unconditional love and help my children have a strong sense of who God has created them to be; and to model living a life of service to God.

• My mission as a mother is to create a warm, welcoming, and peaceful environment in our home; to communicate to each of my children that he or she is deeply loved; to guide each child in developing a strong, growing relationship with Jesus; and to help them each identify, appreciate, and use their unique gifts for God's purposes in this world.

Life Role: Neighbor

• My mission as a neighbor is to develop warm relationships with my neighbors, and to help and serve them in whatever ways I can.

Life Role: Community Volunteer

• My mission as a tutor is to help inner-city young people improve their study habits and grades; to provide encouragement, support, and caring; and to instill the belief that they can accomplish significant things with their lives.

Strategy Two: Setting Priority Goals

Once you have written your personal mission statements, the next step is determining what you need to do to translate your life callings into specific goals. "Goals," said Diana Scharf Hunt, "are dreams with deadlines." We suggest that you take some time to brainstorm and identify possible goals for each of your mission statements. Then select the goals you believe are the most important for you to work toward right now. These are your *priority goals*. Make each priority goal statement:

- *Inspiring* (aim for something you would be excited about achieving as you partner with God; stretch yourself and your faith; push yourself out of your comfort zone)
- *Specific* (create a clear picture of what you want and need to do)
- *Measurable* (determine how you will know when you have accomplished it)
- *Time-limited* (assign dates and deadlines to create accountability, energy, and activity)

Here are two of Jerod's priority goals for his transition from being an engineer in California to a high school teacher living in Illinois:

- I will begin teaching high school math and science in Illinois by September 2000.
- We will purchase our new home in Illinois by July 30, 2000.

Transfer your priority goals to your Life Calling Map. If desired, you can also list the life roles (secondary callings) that pertain to your goals. (See the example on the Sample Life Calling Map.)

Strategy Three: Creating Your Action Plan

Your action plan identifies and orders the action steps needed to accomplish your priority goals. You can develop an action plan that encompasses several of your priority goals, or create a plan that focuses on achieving just a single goal. Your action plan enables you to capture large, God-inspired visions on paper; break your dreams and visions into small, manageable bite-sized steps; and stay energized and motivated by seeing your progress toward achieving your goals and living your calling.

Once you have developed your action plan, transfer your action steps to your calendar each week. Picture yourself completing each step and moving closer to accomplishing your goals. Remember that the purpose of your goals and action steps is to serve you; you do not serve them. This means if a goal or target date needs to be modified, change it! Don't become discouraged if you miss a deadline. Just set a new date and continue moving toward your goal. Even a small step forward brings you closer to accomplishing it.

Here is a portion of an action plan based on Jerod's transition:

Action Plan

Priority goal: I will begin teaching high school math and science in Illinois by September 2000.

Start Date	End Date	Action Steps
3/1	3/8	Compile a list of all high schools within a thirty-mile radius of where we want to live.
3/8	3/15	Contact at least ten teachers and other people I know personally in this area for suggestions and leads.
3/15	3/23	Contact all school district offices in desired geographic area to find out about their hiring process.
3/22	3/30	Send a cover letter and resume to the principal of each school I'm targeting.
4/10	4/18	Follow up each letter and resume with a phone call to the principal.

The Power of Small Steps

"Track + Action = Traction" is Bobb Biehl's equation for change. "A lot of people come up with a beautiful plan," says Biehl. "They have a 'track' laid out . . . in detail but take no action; therefore they get no traction. Others take a lot of action but have no plan; they just spin their wheels. But when you combine a clear plan and take action, you get traction. You begin moving from where you are to where you want to go."[2]

John Wooden, the legendary basketball coach, said, "Do not let what you cannot do interfere with what you can do." His advice is a key for turning your action plan into your reality. Large change is not accomplished in one step; rather, significant change is accomplished by taking a series of small steps. Your action plan outlines the sequential action steps for successfully accomplishing your goals. Break down the action steps to the point where there is an easy step that you can do today.

No step is too small if it is taking us in the right direction. Barbara Sher describes the very distorted picture most of us have about how things actually get done in this world:

> We think that accomplishment only comes from great deeds. We imagine our heroes . . . writing best-selling novels in three months, building business empires overnight, soaring to stardom out of nowhere—and this gives rise to painfully unrealistic expectations of ourselves. And yet nothing could be further from the truth. Great deeds are made up of small, steady actions, and it is these that you must learn to value and sustain.
>
> Often you feel you've done nothing when you've actually done a lot. That's because what you did do seemed beneath notice—it was so small that it didn't "count." But it did—just as each stitch counts toward a finished dress, each brick or nail toward a house you can live in, each mistake toward knowing how to do things right. Directed action, no matter how small, moves toward its point. . . . You'll begin to see how small steps add up.[3]

Your personal mission statements, priority goals, and action plans build a bridge between the vision of your calling in the future and your reality today. It is "hope with a blueprint," showing you where to begin right now. Small steps dispel inertia and create movement. Movement creates momentum. Momentum creates energy. Take the first action step, and you will soon find that your visions have become your life.

Personal Application

1. Complete the activities described in action strategy one: write a personal mission statement for your primary calling and personal mission statements for your four most important secondary callings. Record them on your Life Calling Map: Mission Statements.

2. Develop at least one priority goal for each of your personal mission statements as described in action strategy two. Record your most important goals on your Life Calling Map: Priority Goals.
3. Review action strategy three, creating your action plan. Choose the priority goal that is most important to you and develop an action plan for accomplishing it. Record the steps on your Life Calling Map: Action Plan.

PART SIX

OVERCOMING OBSTACLES TO LIVING YOUR CALLING

11

CONQUERING THE "CALLING BLOCKERS"

There is an eagle in me that wants to soar, and there is a hippopotamus in me that wants to wallow in the mud.
                                                                CARL SANDBURG

Meriwether Lewis and William Clark experienced an "extreme adventure." President Thomas Jefferson sent them on a mission to map the uncharted western areas of North America as far as the Pacific Ocean, and to make "great discoveries" for the United States. In the spring of 1804 they departed from St. Charles, Missouri, and traveled eight thousand miles by foot, horseback, and boat before their celebrated return in the fall of 1806.

They had to prepare for a journey that no one had ever taken before. No maps or travelers' reports existed to help them anticipate what they might face. They figured harsh weather, difficult terrain, and wild animals would challenge them. In addition, knowledgeable people of the time warned them that they might encounter more exotic hazards such as erupting volcanoes and woolly mammoths roaming the land.

In many ways, living your calling is an extreme adventure that no one else has ever been on before. There are real obstacles you will encounter in the world around you. There also may be woolly mammoths that others warn will impede your journey. More often, however, it is internal challenges that you have to confront and overcome if you are to move on in the journey of fulfilling your mission in life.

The Challenge of the Comfort Zone

Getting out of our comfort zone is one of the first obstacles we have to confront in responding to God's call. Having carefully constructed our comfort zone of familiar people, places, things, and habits, we tend to resist anything that threatens our status quo. Pushing its boundaries by making changes in our lives can evoke fear. Uncomfortable with the prospect of feeling anxious, we may resist even thinking about change. Clinging tenaciously to the known, we choose familiarity over risk. The problem with choosing to stay in our comfort zone is that it can come with a terrible price tag—one with eternal consequences. Each time we blockade ourselves further within our comfort zone, it becomes more difficult to hear God's callings in our lives. Jesus never hesitated calling people to leave their familiar lives for the unfamiliar path of following him. Each of us faces the same summons. Even though our physical address may stay the same, God inevitably requires us to change.

Living your calling is possible only if you are willing to hear God's summons and respond in spite of perceived risk. Living the extreme adventure of your calling requires courage, resourcefulness, and willingness to confront new and unfamiliar challenges.

Evidence of the "Calling Blockers"

Getting stuck in your comfort zone can be a sign that you have come up against a "calling blocker" in your journey. Calling blockers are things that get in the way of your seeing who you have been created to be, finding out what you are gifted and called to do, or taking the needed actions to live your calling.

All of us encounter potential calling blockers that can get us stuck or off track on our journey to find and live our calling. They can keep us trapped in a life that is far less than the one God intends for us. What differentiates those who are successful in discovering and living their calling from those who are not is the ability to overcome the calling blockers.

There can be many indicators that a calling blocker is at work in a person's life. For example, some individuals find they are unable to discern the puzzle pieces of their design. They simply cannot identify which skills they enjoy using or what their interests are. They don't know what to do to clear the fog that envelops their God-given design.

Others enthusiastically complete their Life Calling Map but have difficulty envisioning themselves doing something new. Faced with specific steps for investigating new opportunities, they procrastinate to the point of avoidance or attempt to take the steps but find themselves feeling too overwhelmed, confused, or anxious to continue.

Some people complete their Life Calling Map and develop a list of career or volunteer possibilities that are of interest. When the time comes to make a decision, though, they freeze. They become mired in indecisiveness, unable to make a choice. Still others make a decision and develop an action plan. They seem excited about their goals. They unexpectedly discover, however, that they are unable to motivate themselves to take the action steps outlined in their action plan. They become skilled avoiders and procrastinators, all the while feeling upset with themselves and wondering why they can't seem to move forward with the steps that will enable them to accomplish their goals.

When we are wrestling with calling blockers, we resist following through on what God is calling us to do. We may try to rationalize or reshape God's summons: "He couldn't really want me to do *that*. It's too much of a change. Instead, I could stay where I am and do that on the side." Living our calling requires that we face our internal resistance head-on.

Overcoming Your Calling Blockers

Lewis and Clark's expedition encountered snowstorms, seemingly impassable mountains, hunger, fatigue, persistent irritations such as mosquitoes, and life-threatening dangers such as grizzly bears. (They did not, however, come across any spewing lava or prehistoric beasts.) The courageous and resourceful explorers had to meet—and defeat—one challenge after another to complete what has been called a phenomenally successful expedition.

Living your calling requires you to recognize and overcome your own set of obstacles—your personal calling blockers. The next chapters highlight six types of calling blockers, demonstrating how they can get in the way of our becoming the people God created us to be and doing the things he designed us to do. We also introduce strategies for overcoming and transforming those barriers so as to live the life God calls us to live. These "calling catalysts" are tools for overcoming the obstacles in our journey.

As you read the chapters, ask God to help you identify any calling blockers that exist in your life. Ask him to give you the discernment to see any obstacles to obedience, the courage to change, and the power to do so. God has not given you a spirit of fear, but rather "a spirit of power, of love and of self-discipline."[1]

You are not alone in the journey of discovering and living your calling, "for it is God who works in you to will and to act according to his good purpose."[2] With God's help, you can overcome any calling blockers you encounter and complete the journey to which God calls you. Then, at some future time, the One who sent you will deem your life's mission "phenomenally successful."

Personal Application

1. If you see yourself as being entrenched in your comfort zone, what are the benefits of staying there? What are the costs to you of staying stuck?

2. As you worked through this book, were there any places in which you found yourself feeling stuck? If so, what do you think is affecting your progress?

12

FEAR

At the beginning of every act of faith, there is often a seed of fear. For great acts of faith are seldom born out of calm calculation. MAX LUCADO

Our greatest fear should not be of failure, but of succeeding at something that doesn't really matter. AUTHOR UNKNOWN

Entrusted with one talent, the third servant in the Parable of the Talents[1] dug a hole in the ground and hid it out of fear. Most of us can identify with him. Fearful of trying to invest our talents and failing, we may choose to ignore or bury them. But as Jesus told us in this story, hiding our talents displeases the Master. Our talents have been given to us to invest in this world. We may find, however, that we get stopped in our tracks by the powerful calling blocker of fear.

Fear can range from mild anxiety to an icy, gripping, incapacitating paralysis. God knows that we are fearful creatures. John Ortberg says that "the single command in Scripture that occurs more often than any other—God's most frequently repeated instruction—is formulated in two words: Fear not." Ortberg then asks a critical question: "Why does God command us not to fear?"

> Fear does not seem like the most serious vice in the world. It never made the list of the Seven Deadly Sins. No one ever receives church discipline for being afraid. So why does God tell human beings to stop being afraid more often than he tells them anything else?

My hunch is that the reason God says "Fear not" so much is *not* that he wants us to be spared emotional discomfort. In fact, usually he says it to get people to do something that is going to lead them into greater fear anyway.

I think God says "fear not" so often because *fear is the number one reason human beings are tempted to avoid doing what God asks them to do* [emphasis added].[2]

By definition, a God-sized calling exceeds our human capabilities. It not only requires more than we can humanly do but also defies our desire to control, define, curtail, and delineate. Our natural tendency is to become fearful if we don't know exactly what will happen and cannot regulate all of the factors that affect the outcome. We want to be all-knowing and all-powerful, but we're not; those qualities belong solely to God. So it all can seem to be just too much. We stand, shovel in hand, tempted to hide our talents and disregard our Master's mandate.

Fear of Failure

Who hasn't experienced the anxiety of not measuring up to the challenge? Even people who are brilliant in their field fear that who they are is not enough. In the movie *Runaway Jury*, the famous actors Dustin Hoffman and Gene Hackman worked together for the first time. Over dinner one evening, they discovered that each of them was intimidated by the prospect of working together. They both were afraid of forgetting their lines and messing up the scenes. Talking further about their self-doubts, Hackman said, "I don't know about you, but do you know what I feel immediately after a film is wrapped?" Hoffman knew what he was going to say next. "That I'm never gonna get a job again."[3]

Whenever we face something new, unknown, and difficult, all of our fears about our "handicaps" surface. Having provided outplacement services to several organizations, we have listened to many people's fears as they faced finding a new job. Like them, when confronting a scary challenge, most of us tend to create our own litany of perceived limitations and obstacles: "I'm too old . . . too young . . . overqualified . . . underqualified . . . male . . . female . . . too tall . . . too short. . . ." The list goes on. We tend to focus more on what we think we *don't* have than what we *do* have to offer.

Success is achieving a favorable or desired outcome. We all like that. It feels good and we imagine others thinking more highly of us as a result. If something doesn't turn out as we had hoped or expected, it may be seen as a failure. We fall short of our goal. We make a mistake. We blow it. Lack of success feels bad, and we fear others think less of us. We all would prefer to win rather than lose. It is our perspective on failure, however, that determines whether our unsuccessful attempt at something becomes a terminal calling blocker or a catalyst that moves us closer to success.

Results, Not Failure

Henry Ford said "Failure is simply the opportunity to begin again, this time more intelligently." An undesirable outcome can be seen simply as a result instead of a failure. Sally interviewed for a job she really wanted, and it was offered to someone else. She had a choice as to how she would view what occurred. Instead of thinking, "I failed in getting the job," she reasoned: "They thought someone else was a better fit for the position."

Viewing something as a result rather than a failure better equips us to achieve a more favorable outcome in the future. Sally evaluated her performance in the interview and thought through how she might present her abilities more effectively in future interviews. (She even contacted her interviewer to find out if he had any suggestions for her.) Supposed failures do not have to discourage and break us. Instead, they can provide feedback about how to change and develop so we become all that God intends us to be.

Not doing things perfectly is an inherent part of living our calling because we will be growing and doing new things. The key is to see a failure as a learning experience and not as a character trait. Ted Engstrom said, "We must expect to fail . . . but fail in a learning posture, determined not to repeat the mistakes, and to maximize the benefits from what is learned in the process."

Failure Paves the Way for Success

Colonel Harland Sanders tried a number of unsuccessful business ventures. At the age of sixty-five, he decided his fried chicken with its secret blend of eleven herbs and spices was the right idea. He refused to give up in spite of 1,008 sales calls to restaurant owners that ended in rejection. Prospect number 1,009 was the first to say yes. Colonel Sanders said that his faith took him from living off his $105 monthly pension check to running Kentucky Fried Chicken, a $285 billion company.

Max Lucado, best-selling author of more than fifty books, recounts that he had to send his first manuscript to at least fifteen publishers. "Nobody wanted to publish it," he said. He didn't get discouraged enough to quit, however. "Every time I got the manuscript back, I thought, *Well I'll just try another publisher,*"[4] he said. His millions of loyal readers are grateful he did.

Jimmy Carter ran for governor of Georgia in 1966 and lost. Angry with God, he told his sister

> "Ruth, my political life is over! It's not my goal just to grow peanuts, sell fertilizer, gin cotton, and build up a bank account. God has rejected me through the people's vote."
>
> Ruth replied, "Jimmy, you have to believe that out of this defeat can come a greater life."
>
> I responded bitterly, "There is no way I can build on such an embarrassing defeat."

Ruth talked to him about the meaning of James 1:2: "When we face trials with courage, we learn to endure and pray for wisdom. Wisdom leads us to depend on things made available to all through God's love. Christ gives us the courage to take a chance on something new."[5]

Jimmy Carter became the thirty-ninth president of the United States, an active volunteer for Habitat for Humanity, and the recipient of the 2002 Nobel Peace Prize "for his decades of untiring efforts to find peaceful solutions to international conflicts, to advance democracy and human rights, and to promote economic and social development."

Chuck Colson was President Nixon's right-hand man. As one of the major players behind the Watergate scandal, he faced congressional hearings and ultimately was sent to prison. He thought that becoming a felon destroyed his chance of accomplishing anything significant in his life. However, "in the years I've been out of prison, I've seen how God has used my broken experience for His greatest glory. . . . I'm able to do what I do today because of the greatest failure of my life."[6]

Author Madeleine L'Engle had three books published before she was thirty. During the next decade, however, she sold only two new books to publishers, neither of which was a great success. On her fortieth birthday she received yet another rejection from a publisher. She covered up her typewriter and cried. Then she wrote in her journal, "I'm a writer. That's who I am, even if I'm never published again."

She did work on another book, *A Wrinkle in Time*, which was rejected nearly thirty times before it sold. It won the American Library Association's Newberry Medal for Children's Literature and has been read by millions of people. Norman Lear made it into a movie. It was published in 1962; she then sold a new manuscript almost every year for the next two decades. L'Engle says, "Over the years I've worked out a philosophy of failure which I find extraordinarily liberating. . . . If I'm not free to fail, I'm not free to take risks, and everything in life that's worth doing involves a willingness to risk failure."[7]

As these stories illustrate, failure is a natural part of the process of living our calling. The call to use our gifts doesn't come with a guarantee that things will always go as we hope or expect. Our failures, however, teach us lessons we need to learn if we are to move forward. If we are willing to learn, grow, risk, and persevere, past failures pave the way for our eventual success in accomplishing the task to which we were called.

When Plans Go Wrong

Proverbs 16:3, "Commit to the Lord whatever you do, and your plans will succeed," might mistakenly be taken to mean that God guarantees the success of any plan we launch with prayer. Fortunately, this is not the case! Most of us can identify with C. S. Lewis's words, "If God had granted all the silly prayers I've made in my life, where should I be now?"[8] As we make our plans, we do so with the understanding that God may revise them and change us as we move forward.

Andy Stanley gives us this important advice: "Don't confuse your plans with God's vision." His caution is well worth heeding: "Failed plans should not be interpreted as a failed vision. . . . A plan is a guess as [to] the best way to accomplish the vision. . . . I have never met anyone or heard of anyone who accomplished anything significant for the kingdom who didn't have to revise plans multiple times before the vision became a reality."[9]

Our reaction to past failures, unrealized dreams, regrets, mistakes, and our fear of future failures can keep us from becoming the people God created us to be, and from doing the things he created us to do. Most failures are simply the result of being in a learning mode. Some failures require that we confess sin and disobedience before we can move on. God is at work in every facet of our lives, wanting to use all of our experiences to bring us closer to himself. Our part is to trust him and to ask him to show us what we need to learn in order to grow. Our failures may very well become the centerpiece of a beautiful design.

"Calling Catalysts" for Overcoming Fear

Helen Keller wrote, "Avoiding danger is no safer in the long run than outright exposure. Life is either a daring adventure, or nothing at all." Jesus calls us to a life of daring adventure. But how do we deal with our very real fears that tempt us to bury our talents and ignore God's summons? Here are four strategies that can help you overcome your fears and develop the ability to confront any challenges that may come your way as you seek to live your calling.

Strategy One: Stay Focused on Your Personal Mission Statements

If we are inspired by our ultimate aim in life—the big picture of our calling—it is easier to take the necessary steps to reach our goals, even if they seem rather scary. Make a copy of your mission statements and post it on your mirror or refrigerator, or in some other prominent place where you will see it daily. Review the mission statements and remind yourself of why they are important to you. Each day, commit yourself to living in accordance with your personal missions in life.

Strategy Two: Practice Affirming Biblical Truths

Faith is the opposite of fear. The more our minds dwell on biblical truths that build faith and trust in God, the less room there is for fear to become entrenched. Oswald Chambers wrote: "It is the most natural thing in the world to be scared, and the clearest evidence that God's grace is at work in our hearts is when we do not get into panics. . . . The remarkable thing about fearing God is that when you fear God you fear nothing else, *whereas if you do not fear God you fear everything else*" [emphasis added].[10]

The Bible tells us the truth about God, about ourselves, and about what we are capable of becoming and doing in God's power. In the Old Testament, God told his people to "fix these words of mine in your hearts and minds; tie them as symbols on your hands and bind them on your foreheads" (Deuteronomy 11:18).

Clearly, God's intent was that his people stay focused on his Word. That is still his intention for us today. Affirming biblical truths and promises daily is one way of fixing God's Word in our hearts and minds. Reviewing and memorizing verses such as Philippians 4:13, "I can do everything through him who gives me strength," builds your faith and counters fears that may arise. Other possible verses to use as biblical affirmations include Ephesians 3:16, 2 Corinthians 12:9, Ephesians 6:10–11, and 2 Timothy 1:7.

Another idea is to write down each of your fears about living your calling on a sheet of paper. Then, over the top of each of them, write "GOD IS GREATER."[11] God *is* greater than any obstacle you will ever encounter. With him on your side, you have every reason to let go of your fears.

Strategy Three: Don't Expect Perfection from Yourself

Give yourself permission not to do things well the first time (or even several times). When someone is learning a new sport such as tennis or skiing, it takes many hours of practice to develop a level of proficiency. The same is true in other areas of our lives as well.

If you really want to do something and have not yet done it well, determine what you need to do differently in order to succeed. Get additional help or training, if needed. Then keep trying until you are proficient. Each attempt brings you closer to mastery.

Strategy Four: Ask for Support

Your partner or small group can be an important asset in dealing with fear. Many people have accomplished things they thought they couldn't do because someone else believed they *could* do it. Your partner(s) can help you find solutions to obstacles, give you a needed push, and encourage and affirm you even if something you do doesn't turn out quite as you had expected.

If these strategies are insufficient to help you deal with your fears, and you find yourself unable to move forward, consider seeking assistance from your pastor or a qualified counselor. (See strategy two in Chapter Sixteen for suggestions on how to find a Christian counselor in your area.)

Faith Conquers Fear

Fear can be a formidable calling blocker. Faith, however, is ultimately more powerful than fear. Faith is the active exercise of your trust in the God who created you; who owns everything; and who is the sovereign Lord of the past, present, and future. Faith enables you to step out and do what he calls you to do regardless of the risk. Fear will eventually move aside as you continue to move forward in faith.

Personal Application

1. Henry Ford said, "Failure is simply the opportunity to begin again, this time more intelligently." Think of an experience in which you believe you failed. What did you do and think? In retrospect, would you have done anything differently?
2. Choose one of the calling catalyst strategies to help you deal with any fears you may be experiencing about what is ahead for you in living your calling. Record what you do in your journal.

13

MONEY

There is nothing wrong with men possessing riches. The wrong comes when riches possess men.

BILLY GRAHAM

Ken was making a six-figure income as a sales rep for a manufacturing company. A top performer in his company, he had won numerous awards and bonuses for his sales figures. He lived in a nice neighborhood, his children attended private school, and he and his wife drove new cars. The fact that everyone saw him as a success made him even more conflicted about his growing dissatisfaction with his job and his life. Inside he felt miserable and was becoming increasingly depressed.

No longer satisfied with just earning money, he wanted to do something with his life that mattered. "I want to find God's will for my life and career. I just fell into being a sales rep out of college, and although I'm good at it, it just feels empty," he confessed. "I don't want to waste any more time doing something other than what God wants me to do." He said he would be willing to lower his income, if needed, to have a job that was fulfilling and made a difference in people's lives.

After several months of doing career planning, he decided that his gifts could be used best in a career as a construction manager. He had very much enjoyed previous home remodeling projects and had a strong interest in helping to build attractive family homes. Having a sister in a wheelchair, Ken also had a vision of managing projects to remodel homes for the elderly and disabled. He had worked in his dad's construction company during college, so he possessed sufficient knowledge and skills to make a transition. He planned further education and training to become a general contractor in the future. He was confident the job would be a great fit. Enthusiastically, he developed a detailed action plan for his transition.

Several weeks later, however, he hadn't even taken the first action step in his transition plan. During an honest discussion, he admitted he just couldn't follow through on his action plan. Although a career in construction had good income potential, he would not start off at his present salary level. His career change would require adjustments in his family's lifestyle. His wife was vocal about her opposition to his plans. Ken also was struggling with the thought of having less money, fewer "toys," and no longer being seen as well off.

The external and internal pressure became too much. He turned his back on his career goals, telling himself it probably would not have been a good fit in the long run and that it would be foolish to throw away the career he had already established. One of the most powerful calling blockers of all had gotten in his way: money.

The Power of Money

We all can empathize with Ken's struggles. Whether we earn a little or a lot, each of us wrestles with money's hold on our heart and mind. Money is not a neutral thing; it has intrinsic power and the potential of being used for good or evil. God isn't against material prosperity in and of itself. (He did, after all, reward Solomon with extraordinary wealth.[1]) He knows, however, that making prosperity one's life goal can never be enough.

"Accumulating money or stuff is a vision of sorts," acknowledges Andy Stanley. "But it is the kind of vision that leaves men and women wondering . . . wondering what they could have done—should have done—with their brief stay on this little ball of dirt." Stanley warns, "Without God's vision, you may find yourself in the all too common position of looking back on a life that was given to accumulating green pieces of paper with pictures of dead presidents on them."[2]

Living your calling may not require a reduction in your income or major change in your lifestyle. In fact, as your work aligns with your design, you may find that you will earn more money than you ever have previously. The key issue, however, is that God wants you to come to the place where you are *willing* to live on less money if doing what he wants you to do requires it. He wants you to value obedience to him more than money and material possessions.

Money—perhaps more than any other enticement—lures people away from becoming who God created them to be and doing what he designed them to do. Jesus knew that a life focused on money could not be focused on God. He knew how easily money could become an idol in our lives, which is why he talked about it so much. Sixteen of his thirty-eight parables were about how to handle money and possessions. Howard Dayton, CEO of Crown Financial Ministries, said, "In the Gospels, an amazing one out of 10 verses (288 in all) deal directly with the subject of money. The Bible offers 500 verses on prayer, less than 500 verses on faith, but more than 2,000 verses on money and possessions."[3]

Jesus talked about money more often than any other subject except the kingdom of God.[4] Here are some of his teachings that warn about the power of money:

- "No one can serve two masters. Either he will hate the one and love the other, or he will be devoted to the one and despise the other. You cannot serve both God and Money" (Matthew 6:24).
- "Still [other people], like seed sown among thorns, hear the word [of God]; but the worries of this life, the deceitfulness of wealth and the desires for other things come in and choke the word, making it unfruitful" (Mark 4:18–19).
- "Again I tell you, it is easier for a camel to go through the eye of a needle than for a rich man to enter the kingdom of God" (Matthew

19:24). (Jesus spoke these words as he and his disciples watched the rich young man walk away, having chosen to keep his possessions rather than follow Jesus.)

- "Do not store up for yourselves treasures on earth. . . . For where your treasure is, there your heart will be also" (Matthew 6:19, 21).

Jesus' view of money is very clear. Our difficulty is not in understanding what the Bible says about money; rather, our problem is putting into practice what it teaches. Pollster George Barna found, for example, that "desiring to have a close, personal relationship with God ranks sixth among the 21 life goals tested among born-agains, trailing such desires as 'living a comfortable lifestyle.'"[5]

It is one thing to understand God's teachings about the role of money in our lives; it is another to risk being obedient to them. Richard Foster comments on Martin Luther's astute observation, "'There are three conversions necessary: the conversion of the heart, the mind and the purse.' Of these three, it may well be that we moderns find the conversion of the purse the most difficult."[6]

Money becomes a calling blocker when it dulls our sensitivity to God's voice—that is, when it entices us to compromise morally, ethically, or spiritually; or when it so entraps us that we become imprisoned by our lifestyle or our debt. Sadly, money has ensnared many of God's people, their lives illuminating the truth of God's Word: "People who want to get rich fall into temptation and a trap and into many foolish and harmful desires that plunge men into ruin and destruction. For the love of money is a root of all kinds of evil. Some people, eager for money, have wandered from the faith and pierced themselves with many griefs" (1 Timothy 6:9–10).

Learning to manage money wisely is an essential discipleship skill, because it directly affects our relationship with God. We are free to serve God and others fully only after we have put money in its proper place in our heart, mind, and lives.

One of the greatest rewards of our career counseling work has been watching Christian men and women find their vocational callings and then make a successful transition into living them. Conversely, one of

most discouraging things is seeing clients hindered from living their calling by their dreams of wealth and material success, their poor money
management, their excessive debt, or all three.

The Willingness to Trust

For many of us, money represents security. Being free to live our calling
means we have to look to a Source beyond money for our security. We
have to be willing to trust that God will meet our needs. Jesus knows our
human tendency to worry about the necessities of life. In the Sermon
on the Mount, he speaks to our hearts: "So do not worry, saying, 'What
shall we eat?' or 'What shall we drink?' or 'What shall we wear?' For the
pagans run after all these things, and your heavenly Father knows that
you need them. But seek first his kingdom and his righteousness, and all
these things will be given to you as well" (Matthew 6:31–33).

Many of the risks we have had to take personally were financial
ones. Years ago, the journey of living our calling took us to the point
of resigning from our jobs, thus severing our lifeline to guaranteed
salaries and benefits. Soon after, believing that God was calling us to
expand our career counseling work, we signed our first contract for advertising on Christian radio. We committed ourselves to paying an an-
nual fee for advertising that was more than either of us had ever earned
in a year.

Taking financial risks has become easier over the years because we
have experienced God's faithfulness to us. There have been many months
through the years, for example, when we could not pay ourselves because
to do so would jeopardize being able to continue our work. When our
son was born, we reduced our work hours and commitments so we could
be his primary caretakers. But God has never let us down. Over and over
again, we have witnessed his provision for us through new projects and
opportunities. As you take the next steps to which God calls you, you also
will experience God's trustworthiness in new and exciting ways.

Calling Catalysts for Developing a Biblical Perspective on Money

Money is powerful, easily becoming a god in our lives. We must work hard to keep money in its proper place in our lives. Here are some strategies that can help ensure that money is not a calling blocker for you.

Strategy One: Exercise an "Attitude of Gratitude"

Practice gratitude for the material and nonmaterial blessings you already have in your life. Contentment is an antidote for greed. Prior to its warning about the dangers of loving money, the Bible states that "godliness with contentment is great gain. For we brought nothing into the world, and we can take nothing out of it. But if we have food and clothing, we will be content with that" (1 Timothy 6:6–8). Make a list of all the blessings in your life, reviewing and adding to it daily. Thank God for his rich provision for you, and ask him to give you wisdom to distinguish between your needs and your wants.

Strategy Two: Practice Biblical Stewardship of Your Money

Our money—all of it—belongs to God. He entrusts it to us, however, to manage. Most of us will have more than a million dollars pass through our hands during our lifetime, yet many of us will never learn how to manage it well. Our ability to discern and live our calling is directly affected by our ability to handle money.

One of the keys to managing our money according to biblical principles is learning to give money freely. God does not "need" our money; however, giving money serves as a testimony that God owns all things in our lives. One of the first principles of giving found in the Bible is the "tithe," which means "tenth." Giving a tenth of our money to God's work and to meet the needs of others is a voluntary act that is an expression of thankfulness and trust. The Bible clearly mandates that we should give generously and joyfully; for "God loves a cheerful giver" (2 Corinthians 9:7). Opening our checkbook opens our heart and mind to God.

For most people, tithing is a growing edge in discipleship. As one study found, only 6 percent of those who called themselves born-again Christians tithed.[7] The more we learn to be generous givers, the more we will experience the reality of Jesus' teaching: "Give away your life; you'll find life given back, but not merely given back—given back with bonus and blessing. Giving, not getting, is the way. Generosity begets generosity" (Luke 6:38, The Message). If you want to learn more about giving financially to God, are shackled by money problems, or desire to improve your financial management skills, organizations such as Crown Financial Ministries (www.crown.org) offer resources for handling money in accordance with biblical principles. Money has the power to obstruct us in living our calling, or to be used for God's purposes in our lives and the lives of others.

Strategy Three: Develop a "Kingdom Vision" for Your Life

Challenge the American dream by developing a "kingdom vision" in your mind and heart. The American dream of prosperity and material accumulation is so pervasive in our culture and thinking that even those of us who profess to follow Jesus Christ seldom question its rightness. Fresh out of school, we set out to acquire a well-paying job, a nice car, and eventually a house and lifestyle with all the trimmings. Unthinkingly, we seek to emulate our society instead of Jesus.

What is a kingdom vision for life? It is a life that reflects what is important to God. Read through the gospels and see what Jesus says about what really matters in life. (You may want to begin with the Sermon on the Mount, found in Matthew 5–7.) From what you read, make a list of God's priorities for our lives. What does he want us to spend our time doing and becoming? A kingdom vision for our lives is a blueprint for becoming truly rich.

Gaining a Life of Lasting Wealth

The model for our lives is Jesus, not Oprah Winfrey, Michael Jordan, or Bill Gates. The pages of God's Word give us the pattern for our lives, not magazines that portray the lifestyles of the rich and famous. A right relationship with money is possible only when we have a right relationship with God. We must believe that God truly loves us and that he will indeed give us what we need if we seek his kingdom above all else. We must be compelled by a vision of true riches so that we keep earthly treasures in their proper place in our lives. We must also trust that by giving up the life we know we will receive the life for which we have always longed.

Personal Application

1. On a scale of 1 to 5 (1 = not important at all; 5 = most important), how important has the factor of salary been in your making career decisions or thinking about potential careers? How has money affected specific career choices?
2. Imagine that God is calling you to a career in which you will make less money. What adjustments can you make in your life to live on less income? Now imagine that God is calling you to a job in which you will earn twice as much money as you have in the past. What will you do with the added income?
3. If other people reviewed your checkbook register, credit card statements, and cash receipts for the past three months, what would they determine to be your priorities in life given how you spend your money? Are there any changes you think God might be asking you to make in how you manage your money? If so, what are they?
4. Choose one of the calling catalyst strategies to help you address the calling blocker of money. Record what you do in your journal.

14

BUSYNESS

Busy-ness . . . can be a way to avoid God, the meaning of life, and life itself.
SIDNEY S. MACAULAY

We have become a 24/7 society. At any hour of any day of the week we can shop, watch news, be entertained, find information, communicate via e-mail or chat rooms—and work. Many of us feel our lives are 24/7 as well, with our day planners and PDAs (personal digital assistants) propelling us mercilessly from one activity to another. Ask people how they are doing and you will probably get a response like, "I'm really busy."

A recent magazine article[1] chronicled the harried lives of a too-typical, frazzled family. The family's calendar of weekly activities "was so jammed with scribbled entries" that it was difficult even to decipher. The stay-at-home mom described her family's life as "absolutely crazy."

Those of us with school-age children especially can relate to the struggle of deciding how many activities are enough. We hear others talk about their children's involvement in multiple sports activities, music lessons, Scouts, youth groups, language lessons, computer workshops, and advanced academic preparation classes. We don't want our children to miss out or get behind, so we may find ourselves enslaved to a weekly schedule crammed with competing activities.

Presbyterian pastor Coile Estes commented that there is "no such thing as 'sanctuary' in parishioners' lives. Between jobs and families, they have little time for church and less for reflection." Sunday is no longer a day for worship and renewal; children's sports events, birthday parties, and other activities have encroached on the Sabbath. "Families squeeze in on weekends what they have no time for during the week. 'A lot of employers don't appreciate a balanced life,' says Estes. 'I hear that from my people all the time.'"[2] Our days—and those of our children—become frantic and exhausting, leaving little time for relaxing, spontaneous play, church involvement, or unstructured time with family and friends.

Long working hours add to the frenzy of people's lives. "The average workweek is now up to 47 hours, four more than two decades ago. A Gallup Poll [in 1999] found that 44 percent of Americans call themselves 'workaholics.'"[3] Downsizing, mergers, and decreased revenues have created workplaces with fewer workers and increased workloads. Commutes become longer as people work further from home and traffic congestion increases. In addition, both parents work in many families. The Bureau of Labor Statistics reports that 60 percent of marriages are dual-career. Not surprisingly, "lack of time" is cited in one study as the biggest challenge to their marriages.[4]

Too Busy for God

Overscheduled. Overworked. Overcommitted. Overwhelmed. Our busyness can be the product of doing lots of good things. But are they the good things we should be doing? Busyness can be a highly effective calling blocker. When Kevin served on our church's committee seeking to fill church board openings, the most common response to his inquiries about interest in serving was "I'm too busy." A recent poll revealed that "only 10 percent of church members are active in any form of personal ministry." (Encouragingly, however, the poll also found that "40 percent [of church members] have expressed an interest.")[5] God calls us to active service using our gifts within the church, not to a passive and self-centered consumerism in which we focus only on how the church meets our needs. Many of us are missing our callings within the Body of Christ.

Even busyness "working for God" can be a calling blocker. Oswald Chambers urged: "Beware of anything that competes with loyalty to Jesus Christ. The greatest competitor of devotion to Jesus is service for Him. . . . The one aim of the call of God is the satisfaction of God, not a call to do something for Him."[6] Thomas Kelly observed that "too many well-intentioned people are so preoccupied with the clatter of effort to do something for God that they don't hear Him asking that He might do something through them."[7]

Our activity and productivity can prevent us from hearing God's voice and discerning his guidance. How easily we become compulsive people who ignore the Caller while frantically seeking and doing what we imagine (and hope) to be our calling. We are just too busy to consult with the One who calls. Activity, productivity, and accomplishment become our masters. Many of us live our lives as driven people rather than ones who are called.

Driven or Called?

In his book *Ordering Your Private World,* Gordon MacDonald describes the characteristics of stressed, driven people (who often are doing very good things). They are all around us. In fact, often they *are* us! We act as driven people when we

- Value accomplishments and results above everything else
- Seek to acquire things that represent power and status
- Strive for involvement in increasingly bigger and more visible endeavors
- Demonstrate a highly competitive spirit
- Try to impress people with our schedule and how busy we are
- Spend little time pursuing relationships with our spouse, family, friends, and, especially, with God[8]

Drivenness results from listening to the culture around us and the fear inside of us. In his book *When I Relax I Feel Guilty,* Tim Hansel describes our condition of suffering "from a nagging sense of guilt that no matter how much [we] do, it is never quite enough. . . . Words like *wonder, joy, rest,* and *freedom* . . . become faded replicas of what Christ taught. Time becomes a tyrant instead of a friend."[9]

It is indeed easy to become driven. MacDonald confesses tendencies that many of us share: "I look inside my private world, and discover that almost every day I have to wrestle with whether I will be a [driven or a called person]. Living in a competitive world where achievement is almost everything, it would be easy to . . . be driven, to hold on, to protect, to dominate. And I might even find myself doing those sorts of things while telling myself that I was doing God's work."[10] The antidote to these human tendencies is to turn our attention to God's love, grace, and truth. His power within us enables us to exchange our frenetic life of achievement, acquisition, and activity for a life centered on pleasing the Audience of One.

Calling Catalysts for Living as Called, Not Driven, People

Here are some strategies to help invest your time in the things that truly matter to you.

Strategy One: Scrutinize and Re-Create Your Schedule

Take an objective look at the activities you (and your family members) engage in each week. For each, determine the activity's benefits (what you and your family gain from it) and its costs (time and energy required, financial cost, impact on you and your family, and so on).

Evaluate your activities in light of your personal mission statements, priority goals, and action plan. (You may want to do this with someone outside of your family. We often are too close to our lifestyle choices to see them clearly, but a partner or small group can provide helpful insight and feedback.) Address questions such as these:

- Are there any activities I should limit or remove from my schedule because they are hindering me in living my calling?
- Are there any activities I should add? (For example, does your schedule have plenty of time built in for building relationships with your family and friends?)
- Is there sufficient time for deepening my relationship with God?
- Is there time for providing spiritual training for my children?
- Is there time for serving others in my church, neighborhood, and community?
- Is there adequate time for renewal and relaxation?

Modify your schedule according to what you believe God's priorities are for your life. God gives each of us enough time to do all the things he wants us to do. Ask the Lord to help you (and your family) create a schedule that reflects the life he intends you to live. God may very well be calling you to do *less,* not more!

This is not an easy process; you may feel as though you are in uncharted territory. You can begin with a blank calendar and then fill in your highest priority activities first. Write down everything of significance, even if it is an activity at home, such as eating dinner together as a family. Evaluate the importance and impact of each activity you add. Your goal in re-creating your schedule is to use your hours to live the life to which God calls you.

Strategy Two: Take a Daily Vacation

Tim Hansel offers myriad ideas for vacations that bring renewal into our lives. Vacations can be as brief as a minute or two; these "midget vacations" introduce time-outs into our routine that remind us what life is really all about.

Hansel's suggestions for midget vacations include thinking of five reasons why you are glad you're you; making a point to meet someone new before lunch; starting your day by doing something special for yourself; phoning your spouse to say "I love you!"; thanking someone in your office or community for contributing to your life; going on a picnic during lunch; and buying a flower or little gift for someone special in your life.[11]

For one week, try to take at least one midget vacation each day. You might find it becomes a habit you don't ever want to break!

Strategy Three: Commit Your Activities to God

Commit your schedule and intended activities for the day to God each morning. Ask the Holy Spirit to guide you in making wise use of your time that day. Review your mission statements and action plan. Ask God to enable you to live your calling 24/7 each day.

The Great Count Down

The way we spend our days is the way we spend our lives. Let us join with the psalmist in praying, "So teach us to number our days, that we may present to You a heart of wisdom. . . . And confirm for us the work of our hands; Yes, confirm the work of our hands" (Psalm 90:12, 17, NASU).

God gifts us daily with twenty-four invaluable and irreplaceable hours of time to manage. We need the Creator of time to guide us away from living the stressed-out, overscheduled, and anxiety-ridden life of driven people and into living the centered, purposeful, and joyful life of people who are called.

Personal Application

1. Is your life too busy to invest sufficient time living your primary calling? If so, what changes could you make to create more time for developing your personal relationship with God?
2. Do you function more as a driven person or a called person? What would other people in your life say?
3. Use the calling catalyst strategies to help you confront the calling blocker of busyness. Record what you do in your journal.

15

NEGATIVE THINKING

Whether you think you can or whether you think you can't, you're right!
HENRY FORD

What we accomplish in our lives depends, to a large extent, on what we *think* we are able to do. John Homer Miller said, "Your living is determined not so much by what life brings to you as by the attitude you bring to life; not so much by what happens to you as by the way your mind looks at what happens." Many people are hindered in discovering and living their calling by the calling blocker of negative thinking—what has been aptly described as "stinking thinking."

One of the keys to living your calling is learning that you are in control of your attitude. Charles Swindoll has important words for all of us to heed:

> Words can never adequately convey the incredible impact of our attitude toward life. The longer I live the more convinced I become that life is 10 percent what happens to us and 90 percent how we respond to it.
>
> I believe the single most significant decision I can make on a day-to-day basis is my choice of attitude. It is more important than my past, my education, my bankroll, my successes or failures, fame

or pain, what other people think of me or say about me, my circumstances, or my position. Attitude keeps me going or cripples my progress. It alone fuels my fire or assaults my hope. When my attitudes are right, there's no barrier too high, no valley too deep, no dream too extreme, no challenge too great for me.[1]

Each of us has conditioned ourselves to think in particular ways. Our thought patterns become so ingrained and habitual, however, that we don't feel as though we are making choices in how we react to life experiences. But we are. To fulfill our God-sized callings, we need to master our attitude.

Attitude Affects Outcome

Joan sat dejectedly in our office. Her assignment had been to conduct some informational interviews with people who worked as meeting planners, asking them questions about their jobs and the career field in general. When asked how her assignment had gone, she said, "I can't find anyone to talk to. No one is willing to meet with me. I've tried doing this before and I didn't get anywhere then, either. This just isn't going to work." Some gentle probing uncovered the fact that she had become discouraged after not hearing back from the first two people she called. She then decided that the task was impossible and chose to give up.

Interestingly, another of our clients was exploring a similar field. Stephanie, however, had a completely different experience with her informational interviewing assignment. "It wasn't easy because everyone is pretty busy in this type of work. But I kept at it. I knew there had to be a way to find some people to talk to. I had to ask about eight people I knew before I finally found someone who had a good lead. My cousin John knew someone who works at a convention center. John's friend was willing to talk with me, and then he gave me the names of some people he has worked with. So now I've had four informational interviews!" Her positive perspective enabled her to accomplish her goal.

The Power of Self-Talk

Joan and Stephanie bring Henry Ford's words to life. Joan thought she couldn't complete the task, and she didn't; Stephanie thought she could, and she did. They both were right about the outcome. Each woman shaped her attitude—and her eventual results—by the message she gave herself in the midst of the experience.

During all of our waking hours, we have a continuous stream of self-talk going on in our minds. It happens automatically, and we are usually not even aware that we are doing it. Our self-talk interprets our experiences, which in turn shapes our attitudes. Joan's self-talk consisted of "I won't be able to find anyone to talk to . . . no one wants to meet with me . . . this didn't work before and it won't work now . . . I'll never be able to do this." No wonder she gave up! From the perspective she created with her self-talk, it would be a waste of time and energy to continue with an impossible task.

Stephanie, on the other hand, was optimistic that she would succeed. She mentally reinforced messages such as "I know this is challenging, so I'll just have to keep at it . . . I need to be resourceful to connect with people . . . it will be great to talk to people in the field . . . I can do this." Her self-talk created a positive frame through which she viewed her experiences. The first seven people she talked to had no helpful leads for her. Instead of interpreting this to mean "I'll never find anyone to talk to," she framed it as "I'll have to work harder to find contacts."

Reframing Our Experiences

Taking charge of our attitude often means that we have to *reframe* experiences. Reframing is changing the frame of reference we use to perceive an experience. Joan viewed her experiences through the frame of "It will never work, so there's no point in trying." Had she instead been seeing the unreturned phone calls through a frame of "I may have to work at this a while before I succeed," she would have called back or contacted additional people. A negative frame on our experiences and life holds us back; a positive frame motivates us to keep going until we accomplish our goals.

A positive frame on life doesn't just happen, however. We have to create it intentionally moment by moment. Developing a positive, optimistic attitude is challenging. We have to work at monitoring and changing our self-talk, and we may have to reframe how we see ourselves as well our perception of past, present, and future events in our lives. We do have the power to change our lives by changing our thinking.

The Impact of "Basement People"

The people in our lives can affect how we frame ourselves and our lives. You most likely have both "balcony people" and "basement people"[2] in your life. Balcony people are those who cheer you on, affirming your competency and your ability to achieve your dreams. Basement people, on the other hand, are those who have an agenda of cutting you down to size, holding you back, and keeping you stuck. Their mission in life is to pull you—and your dreams—down to their level.

They specialize in saying things like "That's not possible!" or "That will never happen!" or "Are you crazy? You'll never be able to do that!" in response to ideas or dreams you risk sharing. (You quickly learn to keep your hopes, dreams, and ideas to yourself.) They say they are only "encouraging" you to be "realistic" about what you can do in this world. They are always ready to remind you of your limitations, faults, shortcomings, and past mistakes.

Basement people can be actual people in your life: parents, family members, teachers, pastors, and even those friends who negatively influence the way you see yourself and your potential. Basement people can also exist solely in your mind, making up a committee in your head. These committee members repeat (endlessly) the disapproving, judgmental messages you may have heard in your real life. Or they give voice to the doubts and fears you have about your own ability to do something worthwhile with your life. Their messages become part of your self-talk. The more we listen to these basement people, the less capable we feel, and the more our vision of how God might want to use us tends to shrink and dim.

Removing the Bars

We have control over how our life experience and the people in our lives affect us. As Charles Swindoll said, the most significant decision we make each day is choosing our attitude. The more aware we are of the forces we let shape our attitude, the more ability we have to choose an attitude that is empowering rather than debilitating.

The story is told of a small zoo that had a polar bear enclosed in an eight-by-ten-foot cage, which was much too small for its size and needs. Day after day, it paced back and forth as far as each set of bars allowed. One day a zookeeper from a large zoo heard about the plight of the polar bear. He successfully spearheaded an effort to buy the bear for his zoo, which had just completed building a huge, naturally landscaped enclosure with a large pool.

The day came when the bear arrived and was released into its new environment. The zookeeper anticipated the bear would eagerly explore every inch of its new home. Much to his amazement and disappointment, he watched the bear repeatedly pace back and forth, tracing the boundaries of its former eight-by-ten-foot cage. The bars now confining the bear, however, existed only in its mind.

Each of us is the most limiting factor in our own lives. We only attempt what we believe is possible. We need first to see and then remove any bars that reside in our mind so that we are free to envision our God-sized callings. What we do in our lives—or don't do—is a reflection not only of our self-image but also of our faith in God. Shallow faith produces limited results; deep faith produces miracles. Neither our past nor our present hampers God. He can transform and empower you to accomplish *everything* he calls you to do.

Calling Catalysts for Taking Charge of Your Attitude

More than anything else, our attitude—how we think—influences how far we go in discovering and living our calling. Here are two strategies to help you enlarge your faith, change your thinking, and live your calling.

Strategy One: Change Your Self-Talk

Exchange limiting self-talk for motivating messages and positive perspectives on life. We choose how we think and see the world. The Apostle Paul illustrates this truth when he exhorts us to *choose* to rejoice always, to pray with thanksgiving rather than *choose* to be anxious, and to *choose* to think about things that are excellent or praiseworthy (Philippians 4:4–9). Ultimately, the power to think positively comes from having faith in the One with whom all things are possible (Philippians 4:13).

You must *choose* to change any limited-thinking habits you have developed. They won't change by themselves. To get rid of a bad habit, you have to *replace* it with a good habit. Some suggestions are to replace

- "I *can't*" with "How *can* I?"
- "It will *never* work" with "In what ways *can* I make this work?"
- "Yes, but" with "Yes, let's figure out how to do it!"

Trying to think this way may feel foreign, especially if you have well-developed negative thinking habits. You can make major progress just by taking sports psychologist Bob Rotella's advice: "If you don't want to get into positive thinking, that's OK. Just eliminate all the negative thoughts from your mind, and whatever's left will be fine!"[3]

Strategy Two: Share Your God-Sized Callings with Balcony People

Find at least one balcony person with whom you can share your dreams and goals. (If you are not part of a Live Your Calling Group, look for a friend, family member, classmate, work colleague, pastor, teacher, or a person at your church who would be willing to meet with you periodically to support and encourage you.) Hopes, dreams, and perceptions of our callings are often fragile in the beginning. Choose carefully the people with whom you share them. One day, when you are further along in accomplishing your goals, you will be able to tell the basement people in your life what you are doing, and withstand any negativity that comes your way. Who knows? God may use you to change *their* lives!

All Things Work Together for Good

Choosing to see the positive in ourselves and in the life situations we encounter comes down to a matter of faith. Optimism for people of faith is founded on trusting that God is in control; regardless of how bleak or challenging circumstances seem to be, he is using them for our good and his glory.

Personal Application

1. Do you tend to be an optimistic person or pessimistic? Why? How has your attitude affected your ability to discover and live your calling?
2. What messages (positive or negative) does the committee in your head give you about your potential?
3. If appropriate, choose one of the calling catalyst strategies to help you challenge the calling blocker of negative thinking. Record what you do in your journal.

16

CHILDHOOD WOUNDS

Problems do not go away. They must be worked through or else they remain, forever a barrier to the growth and development of the spirit.   M. Scott Peck

Jennifer handed over a list of the career options she was considering. All of them were entry-level positions, far beneath her capabilities and years of work experience. "I just have such a hard time picturing myself being successful doing something I would enjoy," she said. "I've always struggled with my self-image. Guess that's why I've been stuck in my job for seven years. I can't bring myself to believe I would be hired by anyone else to do anything significant."

Greg sat in our office, looking down at his expensive shoes. "I don't know what's going on with me. I make more money than I need. I work more hours than anyone else at the office. I volunteer for every high-visibility assignment that comes along. When I turned forty I started thinking about my job. To be honest, I'm bored by my work, but the thought of doing something less prestigious or making less money seems inconceivable. I feel caught. I don't know why I am so driven."

"The Bible study leader wants me to facilitate one of the small groups," Janet told us. "She says she knows I would be good at it." Janet went on to describe how she felt trapped between not wanting to let the leader down and feeling frightened at the thought of leading a group. "If I don't do well, I'd be humiliated. I really don't want to risk it."

As we counseled these individuals, we discovered that the roots of their current struggles reached back into their childhood experiences. Jennifer's mother was an alcoholic who frequently belittled and berated her during drunken rages. Greg's father was a successful businessman who traveled extensively and spent little time with his son. Janet was an incest survivor. Their sense of themselves, their ability to trust others, and their opportunity to experience normal developmental growth had been affected significantly when they were young.

The Aftermath of Childhood

Our childhood experiences can have an impact on our ability to discover our calling. Growing up is difficult, and many of us get wounded during childhood in one way or another. Some children experience significant trauma, including alcoholism or drug abuse in the home; physical, emotional, or sexual abuse; neglect and abandonment; parental depression or mental illness; religious extremism; divorce; and parental separation or death.

Others may not have had a genuinely traumatic childhood yet find they still bear some scars from family messages they received or difficult experiences they encountered. The aftermath of childhood wounds can manifest itself in many ways in our lives as adults. People who suffered severe childhood trauma in particular may experience some or all of these symptoms, any of which can become a calling blocker:

- Inability to see themselves as valuable, capable, and gifted
- Difficulty determining what they enjoy (often characteristic of a childhood lived in a "survival" mode)
- Drivenness to prove themselves, which may manifest itself in a quest for money, material things, recognition, approval, or power
- Isolation; superficial or dysfunctional relationships
- Distrust of others

- Difficulty trusting God and believing that he loves them, cares about what they need, and desires to be involved actively and positively in their lives
- Procrastination and other avoidance behaviors; difficulty taking action to move forward
- Depression
- Extreme anxiety or fearfulness, overestimation of the degree of risk in a situation, hypersensitivity to perceived danger
- Trouble envisioning a positive future

Sometimes people who unknowingly are struggling with the effects of their childhood experiences blame themselves for their inability to find satisfying work or a sense of purpose in their lives, thinking they are less intelligent or able than others are. Sometimes they blame God for their unhappiness. Confusion, disappointment, discouragement, anger, loneliness, and frustration may characterize their lives.

Calling Catalysts for Healing Past Hurts

If you know or suspect that what happened to you years ago is still affecting you today, we want you to know that you can find help and healing for whatever you are experiencing. God is in the business of bringing wholeness to his children. He wants you to be healed of past hurts so that you are free to love him, love yourself, and love others. He deeply desires for you to discover and fully live his calling for your life. Here are some suggested strategies to help you overcome the calling blocker of childhood wounds.

Strategy One: Learn More About the Type of Trauma You Experienced

Unlike past generations, we live in a time when there are many specialized resources available for helping you better understand the particular type of trauma you experienced, its typical effects, and the steps needed for healing.

Your local library, a bookstore, and the Internet are good places to begin finding helpful resources. A Web search for "children of alcoholics," for example, results in information about organizations such as the National Association for Children of Alcoholics (NACOA), Al-Anon, and related 12-step groups; specific books, articles, magazines, and videos on the topic; and counseling centers that specialize in dealing with this issue.

Strategy Two: Connect with Others Who Understand Your Experience

Regardless of what you have gone through, there are support groups of people (who meet in person or online) who have had similar life experiences. In a group you learn that you are not alone; discover how to find healing; and experience encouragement, caring, and support from others who are on a similar journey. There are also caring and skilled pastors, laypeople, and professional counselors who have been trained to help people who had experiences like yours. There are many resources available to help you move from being a victim to finding healing and wholeness.

If you are interested in professional counseling, two resources for finding a licensed Christian counselor in your geographic area are the American Association of Christian Counselors (www.aacc.net; 434/525-9470); and New Life Ministries (www.newlife.com; 800/NEW-LIFE, or 800/639-5433).

Strategy Three: Get to Know the One Who Loves You Most

Talk to God, even if you feel disconnected from him or angry about what happened to you. Be honest with him about what you are feeling. God loves you more than you can imagine and longs to help you in your recovery. Hold on to the promises found in Scripture:

• "The Lord is a refuge for the oppressed, a stronghold in times of trouble" (Psalm 9:9).

- "He heals the brokenhearted and binds up their wounds" (Psalm 147:3).
- "I waited patiently for the Lord; he turned to me and heard my cry. He lifted me out of the slimy pit, out of the mud and mire; he set my feet on a rock and gave me a firm place to stand. He put a new song in my mouth, a hymn of praise to our God. Many will see and fear and put their trust in the Lord" (Psalm 40:1–3).

You Can Experience Healing

Choosing to examine one's past hurts can feel like an enormous risk with uncertain outcomes. This is why working with someone (such as a pastor or counselor) who is trained to help people with issues such as yours can be an important part of your healing process. Gaining a new level of understanding of what happened to you, and developing new ways of handling its aftereffects, will have a positive impact on all areas of your life.

Personal Application

1. Growing up can be difficult. Are there any ways you see experiences from your childhood or teen years hindering you in discovering or living your calling?
2. If appropriate, choose one of the calling catalyst strategies to help you with the calling blocker of childhood wounds. Record what you do in your journal.

17

GOING IT ALONE

Communion is strength; solitude is weakness. Alone, the free old beech yields to the blast and lies prone on the meadow. In the forest, supporting each other, the trees laugh at the hurricane. . . . The social element is the genius of Christianity.

CHARLES SPURGEON

The giant redwood trees found in northern California and southern Oregon are higher than the Statue of Liberty, towering 250 to 365 feet and weighing more than a million pounds each. They are the largest living things on earth. The trees are between fifteen hundred and three thousand years old, which means that many were alive before Jesus walked this earth. Their longevity is due to a variety of survival strategies, including their unique root system.

Astonishingly, these enormous trees have a root system that is typically only about six to ten feet deep. How is it possible for such a shallow root system to hold up trees of such height and weight? The trees have a twofold strategy: their roots extend over a wide area (often more than a hundred feet) and *they entangle themselves with the root systems of neighboring trees.* The interconnected root systems help individual trees remain stable and upright despite heavy wind and snow.

Entangled Roots

We also encounter many storms—large and small—in life. We need other people so that we can not only survive but also thrive during the ups and downs of life. God especially calls us to entwine our roots with those of fellow believers. As Tim Hansel points out:

> The fact that we are called the "body" of Christ is very integral to this idea. . . . Physiologically, every cell in the body is designed for every other cell. The whole purpose of each cell is to enable all the other cells to perform. The only cell that exists for itself is a cancer cell.
>
> Although the [journey to live our calling] is a personal pilgrimage, it does not require that we be "rugged individualists." The image of the all-American who pulls himself up by his own bootstraps is a totally foreign one to the Christian faith. . . . We're just not built that way, no matter what our world is shouting. We need each other, and when we work with each other, great things happen.[1]

Alone in a Crowd

Even so, many of us find ourselves living an isolated life in which we have few sources of meaningful support. Os Guinness observes that due to our present way of life, "community . . . has fallen on hard times. . . . The plain fact is that for most modern people, community is either a rare experience or a distant, even mocking, ideal."[2] We may long to experience a sense of community with others but feel at a loss as to how to find it.

We wish we could say that our churches are a place where community can consistently be experienced, but that is not the case. Many of our churches are more a reflection of our individualistic culture than of the Body of Christ described in the pages of the New Testament. Though surrounded by others, regular church attendees often experience deep loneliness. Although pastors' lives are full of contact with people, many of them also feel relationally isolated. The Fuller Institute found that "70 percent of pastors surveyed said they did not have a close personal friend."

They report that "they are often too busy to develop close personal relationships of their own."[3] Isolation and a lack of community are calling blockers. Discovering and living the callings God has for us is not possible apart from being vitally connected with other Christians.

A Corporate Calling

In our individualistic view of life, we tend to forget that God calls us both as individuals and as a corporate Body—his Church. A visitor to a local church observed that every worship song that morning used the word *I*: "I exalt You," "I worship You," "I love You, Lord Jesus." The pastor, he noted, used the word *you* throughout his sermon, never *we*. There was no sense of community in the worship, he said; everything reinforced seeing one's Christian faith as a private religion between the individual and his or her God. He commented that it was no wonder that there were so many lonely people in the church, given how the songs and sermons emphasize that we have a "personal Savior" and need to grow in our "individual faith."

He then asked rhetorically, "What would the Church be like if we replaced 'I' with 'we'? If we saw ourselves as a team; an interconnected body of believers; an interdependent community; a family? You can't get *that* from a church on TV."

Each of our individual callings is important as it is a part of God's grand design for his Church. We each have a crucial interconnected role to play in his great drama. God calls us to band with other believers in the journey of finding and living our callings—and supporting them in finding theirs.

One Is the Loneliest Number

Trying to go it alone hinders our ability to discover and live our callings in myriad ways. For example, without a close relationship with other believers you miss out on

- Feedback about your gifts and abilities; opportunities to learn from and be mentored by others in order to grow your gifts; experiences in which you witness how your gifts fit with, contribute to, and are enhanced by others' gifts
- Encouragement in exploring how your gifts might be used in work and ministry; others' ideas and the opportunity for synergistic brainstorming about God-sized visions for your life; sharing of resources and connections in the exploration of possible work and ministry options
- Insightful questioning and wise counsel in making decisions
- Support, accountability, faith-building encouragement; acts of help and service; prayer on your behalf; companionship and comradeship on the journey of discovering and living your calling

The Power of Encouragement

Many people have accomplished what they thought was impossible because someone else believed they could do it. The movie *Stand and Deliver*, for example, portrayed how Jaime Escalante's belief in the potential of his inner-city, underachieving Latino students motivated them to pass advanced placement calculus tests with such high scores that the testing service accused them of cheating.

One of his former students, now a corporate vice president, said, "Today, I continue to enjoy successes which I can attribute to one powerful lesson I learned from Mr. Escalante: 'You can do anything you want to. It's easy; the hardest part is that you have to believe you can do it, and the rest is a piece of cake.'"[4] We members of the Body of Christ need to help one another believe that, together, we can do it.

Calling Catalysts for Getting Connected

Here are two strategies that can help you experience the reality of Christian community.

Strategy One: Connect with Others

Pray that God gives you a desire to be connected with other believers deeply and meaningfully. Ask him to help you find Christian people with whom to be involved. After all, it was God's idea to have the Body of Christ be made up of many members. He knows that we need one another to live our callings. Seek to discern any fears or internal blocks that may hinder your ability to form and maintain relationships with others.

If you haven't already done so, find one or more people (preferably a small group of six to eight people) to partner with you in the journey of discovering and living your calling. (See Appendix A for ideas on how to start a group.)

Strategy Two: Get Involved at Church

Commit yourself to attend a local church and volunteer regularly. The people of God need to worship, fellowship, and serve together to experience the reality of the Body of Christ. If you invest your time, energy, talents, and other resources in the church, you will witness the biblical principle of receiving more than you give.

Strength in Numbers

"Two are better than one, because they have a good return for their work: If one falls down, his friend can help him up. But pity the man who falls and has no one to help him up! . . . Though one may be overpowered, two can defend themselves. *A cord of three strands is not quickly broken*" (Ecclesiastes 4:9–12). Like the great redwoods, we are strong when we are connected.

Personal Application

1. On a scale of 1 to 5 (1= very disconnected; 5 = very connected), how connected do you feel with people in your church, family, workplace, and other arenas of your life? What has contributed to this?
2. What changes, if any, would you like to see in your degree of connectedness with people?
3. If appropriate, choose one of the calling catalyst strategies to help you confront the calling blocker of going it alone. Record what you do in your journal.

EPILOGUE: SEIZE THE DAY

Forgetting what lies behind and reaching forward to what lies ahead . . . press on toward the goal for the prize of the upward call of God in Christ Jesus.

PHILIPPIANS 3:13–14

Professor John Keating (Robin Williams's character in the movie *Dead Poets' Society*) leads his class to the main entranceway of the exclusive boys' prep school. Surrounded by glass cases full of trophies, footballs, and team pictures, Keating directs his students to look closely at the faces of the young men in the photographs.

Like you, he tells his students, those pictured saw a bright future for themselves. But did they, he questions, accomplish even a fraction of what they were capable of doing? Or did they wait until it was too late? Keating reminds his students that these young men are all now dead. There is, however, a legacy they urgently want to pass on. Whispering, he exhorts his students: *Carpe Diem. Seize the day, boys, make your lives extraordinary.*[1]

The Trophies of Eternity

The once-gleaming trophies that fill the showcase rooms of earth become tarnished and covered with dust. Yellow-tinged photographs of victorious teams crack as time relentlessly rolls on. All that remains of many hard-won human achievements in time are mementos and memories of the events in the minds of those yet living. One day, both the mementos and the memories will be gone.

The trophy rooms of heaven, however, know nothing of tarnish or dust. The hard-won treasures there will never depreciate nor be destroyed. Those rooms hold no photographs of long-dead heroes, because the victorious ones are very much alive.

Imagine standing in one of heaven's trophy rooms. You see a beautiful book to which additional entries are being made as you watch. You learn that this is an ongoing record of those who have lived their callings and faithfully finished their work on earth.

The biblical record gives us insight into what God deems to be important in life. Chapter 11 in the book of Hebrews has been described as a "roll call of faith." It lists ordinary men and women whom God heralds as being extraordinary because they exercised faith and committed themselves to obeying his call. Some of the people named had prominent roles in God's great epic; others had but a brief part noted. Yet all were significant in his great sovereign plan.

Entries are being added continuously to the roll call of faith. Looking at the record book of the lives of God's people and reading the summaries of their callings, we might see verses such as these in the pages chronicling recent decades:

- By faith Jim Elliot gave his life to bring the gospel to the Auca Indians. By faith, he based his life on the belief that "He is no fool who gives what he cannot keep to gain what he cannot lose."
- By faith Martin Luther King Jr. sought to set people free from the injustice of racial discrimination. He endured hatred, physical harm, and prison because—by faith—he saw the promised land.
- By faith Corrie Ten Boom hid persecuted Jews and shared the gospel while suffering in Nazi death camps. By faith, she tramped around the world to tell people that "There is no pit so deep that God's love is not deeper still."

- By faith Mother Teresa brought dignity, help, and hope to the outcast, poor, sick, starving, and powerless people around the world. By faith, she taught them the love and forgiveness of Jesus in her words and deeds.
- By faith Fred Rogers used the medium of television to let children know they were loved and valued just the way they were. By faith, he truly loved his neighbor and taught them to do the same.
- By faith Bill Bright began a movement to share the gospel throughout the world and let people know that God has a wonderful plan for their lives. By faith, he chose to be a slave for Jesus.
- By faith Mike Yaconelli served as a prophetic voice of truth to the Church. He sought to equip and inspire young people and those who ministered to them. By faith, he offered the "beautiful mess" of his life to Jesus to use as he saw fit.

There are millions of other names that spark no recognition. These are the men and women who, from a human perspective, lived their callings in relative obscurity. By faith, they raised their children to love the Lord; used their businesses and homes as places of ministry; taught generations of children in Sunday School; gave money sacrificially for the needs of others; and invested their gifts of hospitality, organization, creativity, compassion, discernment, cooking, gardening, building, and countless other abilities in the service of God and others. By faith, they lived their lives for the Audience of One.

Listen for Your Legacy

Those who have faithfully finished their journey on earth before us make up the "great cloud of witnesses" referred to in Hebrews 12. They counsel us to remember what is important in life. From the perspective of eternity, we will waste our lives unless we become the people God created us to be and do the things he designed us to do. Listen to the legacy being passed on to us:

Do you see what this means—all these pioneers who blazed the way, all these veterans cheering us on? It means we'd better get on with it. Strip down, start running—and never quit! No extra spiritual fat, no parasitic sins. Keep your eyes on Jesus, who both began and finished this race we're in. Study how he did it. Because he never lost sight of where he was headed—that exhilarating finish in and with God—he could put up with anything along the way: cross, shame, whatever. . . . When you find yourselves flagging in your faith, go over that story again. . . . That will shoot adrenaline into your souls![2]

What Will Your Verse Be?

In *Dead Poets Society,* Professor Keating asks his students what verse they will contribute to the powerful play of life. The same question is posed to us. God's epic drama of redemption and reconciliation continues, and each of us has the privilege of taking part and adding a verse. In the roll call of faith, what will your verse be?

Look up. The great cloud of witnesses stands near, exhorting you to fulfill your mission in God's great plan. It is not too late to begin. God loves you and wants you to be included in the work of his kingdom. Listen to the voices all around that urge you to accept the challenge to live your calling: *Seize the day. Make your life count for eternity. Walk worthy of your calling because nothing else truly matters.*

Personal Application

1. If your life ended today, what verse would be written beside your name? What do you most want to have written about you on God's roll call of faith when your journey on earth is finished?
2. What have you learned thus far about your own calling? What specific things do you still need to do to discover and live your calling?
3. What are you most grateful for at this point in your journey of discovering and living your calling? If desired, write a prayer expressing your thoughts and feelings.

Check www.LiveYourCalling.com for resources for ongoing support for yourself and your Live Your Calling Group. We want to help you live your calling!

APPENDIX A: LIVE YOUR CALLING SMALL GROUP GUIDE

We have been created to discover and live our calling with others. God does not intend our journey through life to be a solo adventure. There is power in partnership! Therefore, we encourage you to go through this book with a partner or small group. (A group of six to eight people is optimal for a Live Your Calling Group.)

Participating in a Live Your Calling Group will interest people who want to

- Discover their God-given design
- Find their calling within work and/or volunteer ministry and service activities
- Build relationships with people who want to make the most of their lives
- Explore how their faith can be lived more fully in their day-to-day lives
- Experience the adventurous life for which God created them

Getting Started

Here are suggestions for forming a Live Your Calling Group:

1. Draw from your network of friends. Invite one or two of them to participate, and have each of them bring a friend or two.
2. Develop a group from people you see regularly at church, work, parents in your child's "play group," and so on.
3. Create a flyer to post or distribute at churches, bookstores, libraries, college campus career or student activities centers, children's schools, lunch rooms at work, senior citizen centers, health clubs, and daycare centers.
4. Place a notice in the bulletin or newsletter of your church, work, school, or community organization. Invite people to an informal meeting to discuss forming a Live Your Calling Group. (See a sample of a flyer, notice, and invitation at www.LiveYourCalling.com.)
5. Send an invitation to friends, church acquaintances, colleagues from work, family members, and others who you think might be interested. Invite them to an informal gathering to talk about forming a Live Your Calling Group.

Here is how to set up a Live Your Calling Group:

• Your Live Your Calling Group will build community and experience optimal energy and motivation if you meet regularly. The suggested time frame is twelve weeks, with a minimum of one and a half hours for each session for a small group. (Modify the time to fit your needs. Twelve weeks allows time to experience many of the exercises in the book; however, you can go through it in less time. If you have more than twelve weeks, adjust the assignments accordingly. Regarding the length of each session, a two-person partnership may need less than ninety minutes per week; some groups may prefer a longer meeting time.)

• Have group members bring their *Live Your Calling* book and a notebook or journal to the first session.

Format for Group Sessions

Here is a suggested structure for the Live Your Calling Group sessions.

Session One

1. Welcome people to the first session. If desired, open in prayer.
2. Determine together how your group will run. For example:

   Schedule dates, times, and locations for future sessions.

   Stress the importance of confidentiality. Everything that is shared in the meetings is to be held in confidence and not discussed outside of the group meetings.

   As a group, decide whether the same person will facilitate each time or the leadership will be rotated.

   Discuss any other items, such as refreshments, child care during meetings, etc.

   If desired, come up with a name for your group.

3. Have each person share something about herself or himself, responding to questions such as:

   Which activities take up most of your time during the week (work, taking care of family, volunteer activities, and so on)?

   What would you like to accomplish by participating in this Live Your Calling Group?

   What is one thing you really enjoy doing?

4. Point out that there are assignments (listed in this guide) to be completed for each successive session. Ask if there are any questions about the assignments for the next session.
5. If desired, close in prayer.

Here are the assignments to be completed in advance for session two:

- Read the Introduction and Chapters One and Two of this book.
- Respond to the Personal Application questions at the end of each chapter, writing your answers in your journal or notebook.

Session Two

1. Discuss one chapter at a time. Select Personal Application questions to discuss from each chapter, or have each person talk about what was personally most significant from each chapter.
2. Make sure each person gets equal time to share.
3. Ask if there are any questions about the assignments for the next session.

Assignments to be completed for session three:

- Read Chapter Three, which is an introduction to the assessments and the Life Calling Map.
- Complete assessments one, two, and three. Respond to the Personal Application questions that follow each assessment.

Session Three

1. Discuss each assessment (one, two, and three) and its corresponding Personal Application questions separately. As you discuss the assessments, have each person share his or her three most enjoyed transferable skills, top two core work values, and top two preferred roles.
2. Ask if there are any questions about the assignments for the next session.

Assignments to be completed for session four:

- Complete assessments four, five, and six. Respond to the Personal Application questions that follow each assessment, and the "Personal Application section for Part Two" (at the end of the sixth assessment).

Session Four

1. Discuss each assessment (four, five, and six) and its corresponding Personal Application questions separately. As you discuss the assessment, have each person share some of his or her results with the group (the four-letter personality type, top three compelling interests, and one or two spiritual gifts).

2. If you have time, group members can look together at each person's assessment results in the Life Calling Map: Dimensions of My Design to identify any themes or patterns in his or her design (that is, information that is emphasized in more than one box on the map).

3. Ask if there are any questions about the assignments for the next session.

4. Discuss if you want to have a longer meeting next session to allow more time for the brainstorming. You will need a minimum of ten to fifteen minutes per person for the brainstorming, plus approximately forty-five minutes for other group work and discussion. (Therefore, if you have six group members, consider scheduling at least two hours for your meeting.)

Assignments for session five:

• Read Chapters Four and Five; respond to the Personal Application questions in your journal or notebook. Pay particular attention to vision stretching strategy two (brainstorming), since you will be doing this together in your next session.

Session Five

1. Briefly discuss the Personal Application questions from Chapters Four and Five.

2. Conduct the brainstorming activity. To make sure that each person gets equal time, we suggest using a timer set for the allotted number of minutes. When the buzzer sounds, go to the next person right away.

3. After the group has brainstormed for each person, spend some time discussing the activity:

> What are the benefits of brainstorming together?
>
> What did you find to be enjoyable? challenging? surprising?
>
> Have each person share two ideas from the list that she or he finds intriguing.

4. Ask if there are any questions about the assignments for the next session.

Assignments for session six:

- Do one other vision stretching strategy from Chapter Five.
- Read Chapter Six. Respond to the Personal Application questions and complete one vision testing strategy.

Session Six

1. Discuss the brainstorming and other vision stretching strategies you experienced. What worked well? Was there anything you found challenging? Ask for suggestions, if needed, from other group members.
2. Discuss Chapter Six Personal Application questions and the vision testing strategies you tried. Solicit feedback and ideas, if needed, from your group members.
3. Discuss which other vision stretching and vision testing strategies you plan to use to accomplish your particular goals.
4. Ask if there are any questions about the assignments for the next session.

Assignments for session seven:

- Read Chapters Seven and Eight. Respond to the Personal Application questions in your journal or notebook.
- Complete decision-making strategy one, using any career options or volunteer activities you have identified thus far.

Session Seven

1. Discuss Chapter Seven Personal Application questions.
2. Discuss Chapter Eight Personal Application questions and your results from decision-making strategy one. What did you discover?
3. Identify which decision-making strategies you plan to use once you have finished exploring career and volunteer options.
4. Ask if there are any questions about the assignments for the next session.

Assignments for session eight:

- Read Chapters Nine and Ten and respond to the Personal Application questions in your journal or notebook.
- Develop a (rough) draft of a personal mission statement for your primary mission. If desired, choose a personally significant Bible verse to record on your Life Calling Map.

Session Eight

1. Discuss the Personal Application questions from Chapter Nine.
2. Discuss the Personal Application questions from Chapter Ten.
3. Share the drafts of your primary mission statements with one another. Solicit suggestions and assistance from each other, if needed.
4. Discuss the assignment for the next session. Have each group member report to the group the specific activities he or she plans to complete by the next meeting. Encourage each group member to let the group know if there is anything he or she needs from the group in order to complete the activities (such as ideas, contacts, resources, a phone call during the week to provide support or accountability).

Assignments for session nine:

- Complete whichever activities are most helpful to you in accomplishing your goals. For example, if you are working on discerning your vocational calling within work or volunteer activities, you may need to spend time exploring options (Chapters Five and Six). If you believe you have thoroughly explored the possible options, you may be ready to complete the decision-making strategies (Chapter Eight). Or if you have already made a decision, you can move on to writing your personal mission statements, priority goals, and action plan (Chapter Ten).

Session Nine

The structure described in this session is hereafter referred to as the "standard group format." If your group continues beyond twelve sessions, we suggest using this format for each meeting.

1. Determine how many minutes each person will be allotted and set the timer accordingly. (We suggest five to ten minutes per person.) During his or her time, each person then

   Summarizes the goals he or she set in the last session, and what he or she completed during the week.

   Shares what went well, discusses where he or she got stuck (if applicable), and asks for assistance from the group (ideas, information, support, accountability, or problem solving), as needed.

   Specifies the activities he or she plans to complete by the next session. (We suggest that at least one person in the group make a list each week of the group members' goals. Or, each group member can keep an ongoing record of the group members' weekly goals. Knowing what others are working on helps build support and accountability.)

2. Ask if there are any questions about the assignments for the next session.

Assignments for session ten:

- Complete the activities you specified in your group meeting.
- Read Chapters Eleven and Twelve. Respond to the Personal Application questions in your journal or notebook.

Session Ten

1. Use the standard group format (as outlined in session nine).
2. Discuss the Personal Application questions from Chapters Ten and Eleven.
3. Ask if there are any questions about the assignments for the next session.

Assignments for session eleven:

- Complete the activities you identified in your group meeting.
- Read Chapters Thirteen through Seventeen. Respond to the Personal Application questions in your journal or notebook.

Session Eleven

1. Use the standard group format.
2. Have group members discuss any points from Chapters Thirteen through Seventeen they found particularly meaningful or significant.
3. Plan for a time of celebration during the next session. (You might want to have a potluck meal or a dessert buffet.) Ask if there are any questions about the assignments for the next session.
4. Discuss the possibility of the group continuing to meet after the next session. Ongoing meetings—whether with the whole group or a portion of it—provide group members with continued support, encouragement, and accountability in taking the action steps needed to discover and live their calling.

Assignments for session twelve:

- Complete the activities you identified in your group meeting.
- Read the Epilogue. Respond to the Personal Application questions in your journal or notebook.
- Prepare to share about your experience of the past twelve weeks. For example, think about such questions as:

  > What were my goals at the beginning of the twelve-week session? What have I accomplished thus far?

  > What have I learned about God in the past weeks? How have I experienced his being involved in my journey?

  > What are the two most significant things I have discovered about my calling? (If desired, bring a collage, picture, or a poem you have created, or anything else that symbolizes something about your calling.)

  > What are the next action steps I need to take to continue the journey of living my calling?

Session Twelve

1. Set the timer for ten to fifteen minutes (or whatever period of time your group chooses) so that each person has equal time to share about his or her experience during the last twelve weeks. You may also want to ask group members to share their responses to one or more of the Personal Application questions from the Epilogue section.

2. Discuss whether your Live Your Calling Group will be continuing. We suggest interested group members commit to an additional four to eight weeks, and then evaluate at that time if they want to continue longer. Determine where and when you will meet for your next session.

3. If desired, close in a time of prayer. The group may want to pray for each member individually.

Ongoing Sessions

Use the standard group format as the primary structure for your meetings. Schedule periodic times to evaluate the progress you are making in living your calling and celebrate what God is doing in your lives!

APPENDIX B: HOW TO USE THE *OCCUPATIONAL INFORMATION NETWORK (O*NET)* AND THE *OCCUPATIONAL OUTLOOK HANDBOOK (OOH)* TO EXPLORE CAREER OPTIONS

The Occupational Information Network—O*NET—*[is] the nation's primary source of occupational information. The* O*NET *database . . . will help . . . employers, workers, educators, and students make informed decisions about education, training, career choices, and work. The* O*NET *Project is administered and sponsored by the US Department of Labor's Employment and Training Administration.* THE OCCUPATIONAL INFORMATION NETWORK RESOURCE CENTER

As described in Chapter Five, the *O*NET (Occupational Information Network)* online database and the *Occupational Outlook Handbook (OOH)* are two helpful career resources for finding work options that fit your design. Without your Life Calling Map, however, these resources can be overwhelming. Your map helps direct you to the right areas to explore.

For those readers who desire to use the *O*NET* and *OOH* systematically, we suggest these steps to connect the information in your Life Calling Map: Dimensions of My Design with specific career options.

1. Go to *O*NET OnLine* (http://online.onetcenter.org). Click on "Find Occupations." You will see a drop-down list entitled "By Job Family or All Occupations." This is the list you will use to navigate through the *O*NET* site.

2. Look at your Life Calling Map and remind yourself of your top skill cluster categories. Then review Table 5.1 in this book, which shows how your skill cluster categories relate to the *O*NET* job families. On your copy of Table 5.1, mark the job families you want to explore.

3. Click on a job family of interest. You will see a list of job titles. On the right side of the screen you also see a section called "Reports." Most of the job titles have a link for "Details" within the reports section.

4. Find a job title of interest. Click on the details link. We suggest that you focus on the "Tasks" section. (There are several categories of information listed for each job: tasks; knowledge, skills, abilities, work activities, work context, job zone, interests, work values, work needs, related occupations, and wages and employment. Our suggestion is that, at least initially, you not read through all of it. Doing so slows you down in getting a big-picture look at options in the world of work and, for many people, is rather overwhelming.)

5. The tasks section lists the transferable skills used in each job. Compare your list of transferable skills you enjoy using (from your Life Calling Map) with the skills that are used in the job. The skill names may not be an exact match, but you can easily see if the types of skills listed are ones that are of interest to you.

6. Compare each job of potential interest with the information in your Life Calling Map. Take brief notes about each job that is of some interest to you. The worksheet for evaluating job options (Table 5.2) provides a format for taking notes.

When taking notes on a job, first write down the job title, *O*NET*-SOC code, and job family (so you can find the job again, if needed); then, comparing the description of the job with your Life Calling Map, summarize the parts of the job that fit you and make it of interest, note any parts of the job that are not of interest to you, and jot down any questions or comments you have about the job. Aim to take notes on at least twenty or more jobs that are of some interest.

7. Once you feel you have taken notes about each job of interest in the *O*NET*, you can use the *OOH*, which can be found at www.Christian CareerCenter.com in the Career Exploration section, to read more about many of the jobs. For each of the 250 jobs described (listed alphabetically for easy navigation), it addresses the nature of the work, future employment outlook, earnings, related occupations, training and advancement, employment opportunities, and sources of additional information.

8. Review the notes you took about jobs of interest, and mark the six to ten jobs of *most* interest to you. (Chapter Six contains strategies for gathering additional information and testing these options further to see how well they fit your design.)

APPENDIX C: RESOURCES FOR LIVING YOUR CALLING

Visit www.LiveYourCalling.com

Join the online community of people who want encouragement and resources for discovering and living their calling. Sign up for the free online newsletter. Find suggestions and resources to start or join a Live
Your Calling Group for ongoing support and accountability.

Grow in Your Relationship with God

Among the excellent resources for strengthening the spiritual foundations of your life and helping you keep your primary calling primary
are the following:

- *Celebration of Discipline: The Path to Spiritual Growth,* by Richard Foster,
is considered by many to be the best modern book on Christian spirituality. Foster explores the "classic Disciplines," or central spiritual practices,

of the Christian faith. He explains how the disciplines are the means by we which experience spiritual growth and a balanced Christian life.

• *The Life You've Always Wanted,* by John Ortberg, offers a contemporary perspective on the Christian spiritual disciplines. He shows how God uses them to transform us so our lives are "filled with new meaning, hope, change, and a joyous, growing closeness to Christ."

• *The Purpose-Driven Life: What on Earth Am I Here For?* by Rick Warren, explores five God-ordained purposes in life—worship, fellowship, discipleship, ministry, and mission—and shows how they provide the keys to effective living.

• RENOVARÉ can help you on your journey by providing a balanced vision and a practical strategy for the formation of Christlike character. See www.Renovare.org for information about resources and conferences (303-792-0152).

• Christ@Work, a member of the FCCI/Crown Financial Ministries Family, (www.fcci.org; 405-917-1681), and Marketplace Leaders (www.marketplaceleaders.org; 678-455-6262) can assist you in living your primary calling in the workplace.

• *The International Faith & Work Directory* (edited by Mike McLoughlin, Neal Johnson, Os Hillman, and David W. Miller) has more than twelve hundred listings for nonprofit workplace ministries, businesses, churches, and colleges that emphasize the faith and work mission. Find organizations in your geographic area. (Available through www.marketplaceleaders.org)

Find Work That Fits Your God-Given Design

These Websites offer a variety of valuable resources to assist you in living your vocational calling:

• The Christian Career Center (www.ChristianCareerCenter.com). The mission of this online "one-stop" career center is to help men and women integrate their faith with career and life planning and find work that fits their God-given design. Resources to help you find your vocational calling include the free Career Check-Up Inventory (to assess how well your current job fits you), a Job Bank, Job Fair, Resume Bank, career testing and guidance, job search assistance, free articles, and career resources.

• Church Jobs Online (www.ChurchJobsOnline.com). This is a division of the Christian Career Center. Church Jobs Online is a simple and effective way for churches to find quality employees, and for pastors and other church professionals to find new ministry positions.

• The Riley Guide (www.rileyguide.com). This resource offers a directory of employment and career information sources and services on the Internet.

NOTES

Chapter One: In Search of a Calling

1. Kruger, P. "Betrayed by Work." *Fast Company,* Nov. 1, 1999, p. 182.
2. Guinness, O. *The Call.* Nashville, Tenn.: Word, 1998, pp. 40–41.
3. "In the New Testament, there are three instances of the call to a specific role or task: (1) God's call of Paul to be an apostle (Romans 1:1; 1 Corinthians 1:1); (2) God's call of Barnabas and Saul to be the Church's first missionaries (Acts 13:2); and (3) God's call to Paul and his companions to take the gospel to Macedonia (Acts 16:9–10). However, careful examination of these examples along with the rest of the New Testament reveals that they are the exception rather than the rule." Friesen, G. *Decision Making and the Will of God.* Portland, Oreg.: Multnomah Press, 1980, p. 313.
4. Os Guinness introduces this helpful term in his book, *The Call,* p. 31.
5. 1 Corinthians 1:9. Other verses that describe our primary calling to a relationship with God include the following:

   Romans 1:6: "And you also are among those who are *called* to belong to Jesus Christ" [emphasis added].
   Jude 1: "To those who have been *called,* who are loved by God the Father and kept by Jesus Christ."
   1 Timothy 6:12: "Fight the good fight of the faith. Take hold of the eternal life to which you were *called* when you made your good confession [of faith in Jesus Christ] in the presence of many witnesses."

   To learn more about how to have a personal relationship with God, see "Your Most Important Calling" on our Website, www.LiveYourCalling.com.

6. John 1:12–13.
7. 2 Corinthians 5:17.
8. Verses that describe our calling to discipleship include the following:

2 Timothy 1:9: "[God] has saved us and *called* us to a holy life—not because of anything we have done but because of his own purpose and grace" [emphasis added].

Galatians 5:13: "You . . . were *called* to be free. But do not use your freedom to indulge the sinful nature; rather, serve one another in love."

Colossians 3:15, 17: "Let the peace of Christ rule in your hearts, since as members of one body you were *called* to peace. And be thankful. . . . And whatever you do, whether in word or deed, do it all in the name of the Lord Jesus, giving thanks to God the Father through him."

9. Ephesians 4:1 (NKJV).
10. Willard, D. *The Divine Conspiracy: Rediscovering Our Hidden Life in God.* San Francisco: HarperSanFrancisco, 1998, p. 283.
11. Paraphrase of a portion of Ephesians 2:10 attributed to G. Campbell Morgan on a greeting card. *Roy Lessin's Signature Collection.* Siloam Springs, Ark.: DaySpring Cards.
12. 1 Corinthians 3:9.
13. Guinness (1998), p. 31.
14. Maxwell, J. "Johnny Hart: Not Caving In." *Christian Reader,* Mar.-Apr. 1997, p. 18.
15. 2 Corinthians 12:9.
16. Maxwell (1997).
17. Wood, G. "Mission Delayed." *Christian Reader,* Jan.-Feb. 2000, p. 44.
18. Matthew 20:1–16.
19. Matthew 20 (The Message).
20. Quote from Willard, D. "Workbook," RENOVARÉ Regional Conference on Spiritual Growth, Feb. 2003, p. 3.
21. Willard, D. *Renovation of the Heart.* Colorado Springs: NavPress, 2002, p. 194.
22. Jeremiah 29:11.

Chapter Two: Called to Be You

1. For our navigationally astute readers, please note that in using this metaphor we are not making a distinction between technical differences such as "true north" and "magnetic north."
2. Lewis, C. S. *Mere Christianity.* New York: Macmillan, 1952, p. 189.
3. See, among other verses, Ephesians 4:22–24; 2 Corinthians 3:18; and Colossians 3:10.
4. O'Connor, E. *Eighth Day of Creation.* Waco, Tex.: Word Books, 1971, p. 15.
5. 1 Peter 4:10.
6. Buechner, F. *Wishful Thinking: A Theological ABC.* San Francisco: HarperSanFrancisco, 1993, p. 95.
7. Stanley, A. *Visioneering.* Sisters, Oreg.: Multnomah, 1999, pp. 225–226.
8. Luke 12:48.
9. Bishop, R. "Karole Shirley: Giving the Gift of Work." *Christian Reader,* Mar.-Apr. 1998, p. 61.
10. Ephesians 2:10.

11. Matthew 19:26.
12. 2 Corinthians 3:18.
13. Ephesians 3:20 (The Message).

Chapter Three, Assessment Four: Personality Type

1. In this part of the chapter, we present a checklist of typical characteristics for each of the preferences. Please see our Website (www.LiveYourCalling.com) for information on how you can take the actual Myers-Briggs Type Indicator® instrument (as well as other career assessments) and have a professional counselor interpret and discuss your results with you.

     The descriptions of the preference scales and the sixteen temperament types were taken and adapted from these resources and used by permission:

     Martin, C. *Looking at Type™: The Fundamentals.* Gainesville, Fla.: Center for Applications of Psychological Type, 1997.

     Martin, C. *Looking at Type and Careers.* Gainesville, Fla.: Center for Applications of Psychological Type, 1995.

Chapter Three, Assessment Six: Spiritual Gifts

1. Wagner, P. *Your Spiritual Gifts Can Help Your Church Grow.* Ventura, Calif.: Regal Books, 1994, p. 52.
2. Lotz, A. G. *Just Give Me Jesus.* Nashville, Tenn.: W Publishing Group, 2000, pp. 170–171.
3. Wagner (1994), p. 68.

Chapter Four: Picturing Possibilities for Your Life

1. John 6:1–14.
2. Hybels, B. "5 Things Leaders Do." *LeadershipJournal.net,* Sept. 9, 2003. (http://www.christianitytoday.com/leaders/)
3. Guinness (1998), pp. 187, 188, 192.
4. Stanley (1999), p. 225.
5. Dobson, J. "Twenty-Five Years of God's Faithfulness." *Dr. Dobson's Newsletter,* July 2002. (http://www.family.org/docstudy/newsletters/a0021301.cfm)
6. For more information on Michael's work and Wycliffe Bible Translators, visit http://www.worldforchrist.org/races/missionwork/.
7. Chambers, O., and Reimann, J. (ed.). *My Utmost for His Highest: 365 Daily Devotional.* Chicago: Moody, 1997, Jan. 25 entry.
8. Stanley (1999), p. 42.

Chapter Five: Toolbox of Strategies
for Stretching Your Vision

1. Burgess, D. F. (compiler). *Encyclopedia of Sermon Illustrations.* St. Louis: Concordia, 1988, p. 64.

Chapter Six: Toolbox of Strategies
for Testing Your Visions

1. See our Website (www.ChristianCareerCenter.com) for more detailed information on how to find contacts, set up, and conduct informational interviews.

Chapter Seven: Partnering with God
in Decision Making

1. Willard (1998), pp. 203–204.
2. Waltke, B. *Finding the Will of God: A Pagan Notion?* Grand Rapids, Mich.: Eerdmans, 1995, p. 143.
3. See Acts 16:7 and 20:22.
4. See Acts 16:3–5, 19:21, and 20:16; and Titus 3:12.
5. Smith, G. T. *Listening to God in Times of Choice: The Art of Discerning God's Will.* Downers Grove, Ill.: InterVarsity Press, 1997, p. 14.
6. Smith, M. B. *Knowing God's Will: Finding Guidance for Personal Decisions.* Downers Grove, Ill.: InterVarsity Press, 1991, pp. 59–60.
7. "Beth Moore." *Today's Christian Woman,* July-Aug. 2003, p. 66. (http://www.christianity today.com/tcw/2003/004/18.66.html)
8. Swindoll, C. *The Mystery of God's Will.* Nashville, Tenn.: Word, 1999, p. 34.
9. Waltke (1995), p. 148.
10. Staub, D., and Trautman, J. "Biblical Foundations." In *The Career Kit: A Christian's Guide to Career Building.* Seattle: Intercristo,1985, p. 29.
11. Sine, T., and Sine, C. *Living on Purpose: Finding God's Best for Your Life.* Grand Rapids, Mich.: Baker Books, 2002, p. 77.
12. See Acts 14:27, 1 Corinthians 16:8–9, and 2 Corinthians 2:12–13.
13. Friesen (1980), p. 221.
14. Hebrews 4:12.
15. John 14:26.
16. Warren, R. *The Purpose-Driven Life.* Grand Rapids, Mich.: Zondervan, 2002, p. 286.
17. Wales, K. "Christy: In the Fullness of Time," 1995. (http://members.tripod.com/~ Constance_2/fight.html)
18. Wooding, D. "Four New Christian Films from Ken Wales." *Bible Network News,* Apr. 3, 2002. (http://www.biblenetworknews.com/cgi-gin/pfp.cgl?bottom=self)

Chapter Nine: Planning Your Journey

1. Franklin, K. "Creative Befuddlement." *Tucson Weekly,* Jan. 29, 1998. (www. tucsonweekly.com)
2. Mark 4:19.
3. Covey, S. *The 7 Habits of Highly Effective People.* New York: Simon & Schuster, 1989, p. 97.
4. Hansel, T. *Holy Sweat.* Waco, Tex.: Word Books, 1987, p. 88.
5. Covey, S. *First Things First.* New York: Simon & Schuster, 1994, p. 155.
6. Ziglar, Z. *Over the Top.* Nashville, Tenn.: Thomas Nelson, 1994, p. 184.
7. Ziglar (1994), pp. 160–161.
8. Hansel (1987), p. 92.
9. Engstrom, T. *Pursuit of Excellence.* Grand Rapids, Mich.: Zondervan, 1982, p. 23.
10. Kallestad, W. *Wake Up Your Dreams.* Grand Rapids, Mich.: Zondervan, 1996, p. 189.
11. James 2:17.
12. Knorr, M. "Find Your Lost Sense." *Backpacker,* Feb. 2000. (www. Backpacker.com)

Chapter Ten: Toolbox of Strategies for Living Your Calling

1. Chambers and Reimann (1997), February 20 entry.
2. Biehl, B. *Masterplanning.* Nashville, Tenn.: Broadman and Holman, 1997, p. 18.
3. Sher, B. *Wishcraft.* New York: Ballantine, 1979, p. 106.

Chapter Eleven: Conquering the "Calling Blockers"

1. 2 Timothy 1:7
2. Philippians 2:13

Chapter Twelve: Fear

1. Matthew 25: 14–30.
2. Ortberg, J. *If You Want to Walk on Water, You've Got to Get out of the Boat.* Grand Rapids, Mich.: Zondervan, 2001, pp. 117–118.
3. *Runaway Jury* (DVD). Los Angeles: Fox Home Entertainment. Release date: Feb. 17, 2004. Scene-specific commentary by Gene Hackman and Dustin Hoffman.
4. Maxwell, J. *Your Road Map for Success.* Nashville, Tenn.: Thomas Nelson, 2002, p. 127.
5. Carter, J. *Living Faith.* New York: Random House, 1996. (www.preachingtoday.com)
6. *Union News and Information.* Jackson, Tenn.: Union University, Oct. 4, 2002. (http://www.uu.edu/news/newsreleases/release.cfm?ID=438)

7. (http://www.sermonillustrator.org/illustrator/sermon2b/madeleine_l'engle.htm)

8. Lewis, C. S. *Letters to Malcolm: Chiefly on Prayer.* London: Geoffrey Bles, 1964.

9. Stanley (1999), p. 156.

10. Chambers, O., Chambers, B., and McCasland, D. *The Complete Works of Oswald Chambers.* Grand Rapids, Mich.: Discovery House, 2000.

11. Adapted from an exercise in Coyle, N. *Free to Dream.* Minneapolis: Bethany House, 1990.

Chapter Thirteen: Money

1. See 1 Kings 3:13.

2. Stanley (1999), pp. 14–15.

3. Dayton, H.L., Jr. *Leadership,* vol.2, no. 2. (http://www.preachingtoday.com)

4. Foster, R. *The Challenge of the Disciplined Life.* San Francisco: HarperSanFrancisco, 1985, p. 19.

5. Lobdell, W. "Pollster Prods Christian Conservatives." *Los Angeles Times,* Sept. 14, 2002, p. B22.

6. Foster (1985), p. 19.

7. Hansen, C. "The Ancient Rise and Fall of Tithing." *Christianity Today,* June 5, 2003. (http://www.christianitytoday.com/history/newsletter/2003/jun6.html)

Chapter Fourteen: Busyness

1. Renkl, M. "The Frazzled Family Makeover." *Ladies' Home Journal,* May 2003, p. 58.

2. Morris, B. "Is Your Family Wrecking Your Career?" *Fortune,* Mar. 17, 1997.

3. Editors. "No Time to Slow Down." *U.S. News & World Report,* June 26, 2000, p. 14.

4. "Two Careers, One Marriage—Making It Work in the Workplace: A Catalyst Study of Dual-Career Couples." May 29, 2002. (http://www.skillcircle.com/resources/articles/2949.html)

5. *How to Run the Alpha Course: The Director's Handbook.* London: Alpha International, 2001, p. 16.

6. Chambers and Reimann (1997), Jan. 18 entry.

7. Kelly, T. *A Testament of Devotion.* New York: HarperColllins, 1941, p. 97.

8. MacDonald, G. *Ordering Your Private World.* Chicago: Moody Press, 1984, pp. 33–37.

9. Hansel, T. *When I Relax I Feel Guilty.* Elgin, Ill.: David C. Cook, 1979, pp. 12–13.

10. MacDonald (1984), p. 65.

11. Hansel (1979), pp. 131–138.

Chapter Fifteen: Negative Thinking

1. Swindoll, C. *Strengthening Your Grip.* Nashville, Tenn.: W. Publishing Group, 1982, pp. 206–207. Used by permission of Insight for Living, Plano, Texas 75026.

2. Terms used by Joyce Landorf Heatherly in Landorf, J. *Balcony People.* Nashville, Tenn.: Word, 1985.

3. Maxwell, J. *Thinking for a Change.* New York: Time Warner, 2003, pp. 164–165.

Chapter Seventeen: Going It Alone

1. Hansel (1987), p. 106.
2. Guinness (1998), pp. 98–99.
3. Chung, L. "Pastors Burn Out, Too." *Wisconsin State Journal,* Sept. 22, 1993, p. 1.
4. "Jaime Escalante 1999 Inductee." The National Teachers Hall of Fame, Oct. 6, 2003. (http://www.nthf.org/escalante.htm)

Epilogue: Seize the Day

1. *Dead Poets Society.* Original screenplay by Tom Schulman. Burbank, Calif.: Touchstone Video, 1989.
2. Hebrews 12:1–3 (The Message).

TELL US YOUR STORY!

We would love to hear from you! Please write and tell us how you have used this book in your life.

- What are you now doing differently?
- What changes have you made in your life?
- How have you been affected spiritually?
- What tips and suggestions do you have that we can share with others?
- If you are involved with a Live Your Calling Group, what has your experience been like?

Share your success stories with us. Thank you!

Kevin and Kay Marie Brennfleck
www.LiveYourCalling.com
e-mail: Info@LiveYourCalling.com

ACKNOWLEDGMENTS

Encouragement is a powerful force that has fueled our writing of this book. We are indebted to the "balcony people" in our lives who saw the potential of this project and offered words of encouragement that inspired and heartened us during the long, challenging journey of bringing this book into being. We would especially like to thank:

- Mark Kerr, former editor with Jossey-Bass, who shared our vision for this book and introduced us to the publishing business with patience and graciousness.
- Julianna Gustafson, Catherine Craddock, Andrea Flint, and Sandy Siegle, who shepherded this project through the publication process at Jossey-Bass. We appreciate their professional competency, responsiveness to our questions, and personal warmth.
- Marita Littauer, Florence Littauer, and the staff and "extended family" of CLASS (Christian Leaders, Authors, and Speakers Services). They opened the door into the publishing world for us and prepared us to walk through it.

- Our clients, who invited us into their lives and trusted us to help shape their journey of discovering and living their callings. Thank you to those whose stories are told in this book, and to all the others whose lives have contributed to what we have learned and shared in these pages.

- Our manuscript reviewers: Philip Carlson, Mitties DeChamplain, Jim and Jan Holsclaw, Jamie Johnson, Lynn Pearson, Rick Rupp, Bill and Joyce Shannon, and Todd Shinabarger. They invested much time, thought, expertise, and energy in reading the first manuscript; offered invaluable comments and perspectives; and conveyed their enthusiasm about the book. Our thanks also go to Dana Alexander for his encouraging feedback during the last stages of revising the manuscript.

- Tom Dalton, who invested many hours beyond his review of our first manuscript helping us refine our ideas and writing. During the final months of writing, his belief in the value of the project and his sense of humor helped sustain us.

- The Cornerstone class and our small group from Bethany Church of Sierra Madre, and the other friends and family who lifted up this project in prayer. We know that any parts of this book that are deemed to be of value were shaped by their intercession.

- Carole Carlson, Brandy Wells, and our other dear friends who helped us balance our calling to parenthood with the calling to write this book.

- Our children, Brian and Amy, who patiently shared us with this book project for more than two years.

- Kay Marie's parents: Lowell L. Jett, who gave the best he had to give as a father; and Carol Johnson Jett, who in eleven brief years gave me the foundation upon which to build my life.

- Kevin's parents and sisters: Ralph Brennfleck, who has been, and continues to be, a model of faithfulness in living his calling as a father, friend, and follower of Jesus Christ; Myrtle Brennfleck, who lived her calling as my mother by believing in my potential and encouraging me to become the person God created me to be; Gail Angliss, who teaches inner-city children and is an example of investing oneself to meet the needs of others; and Joyce Shannon, for modeling how to balance multiple callings in her roles as a minister's wife, homeschooling mother, and editor.

• Jesus Christ, who fulfilled his mission on earth thus making it possible for all of us to fulfill our mission in life.

THE AUTHORS

Kevin Brennfleck and **Kay Marie Brennfleck** are career counselors and life calling coaches who have a passionate interest in helping people find their purpose in life. They are National Certified Counselors (NCC) and National Certified Career Counselors (NCCC), with many years' experience assisting people through individual counseling and coaching, workshops, outplacement programs, and retreats. They have provided programs and services for such organizations as Insight for Living, World Vision, FaithWorks, World Impact, Campus Crusade for Christ, Wycliffe Bible Translators, and the Christian Management Association (CMA), as well as many Christian schools and churches.

Their Websites (www.LiveYourCalling.com, www.ChristianCareer Center.com, and www.ChurchJobsOnline.com) offer a variety of resources and services and currently receive more than one million hits per month. The Brennflecks find great joy in equipping people to partner with God in the journey of discovering and living their calling.

The Anger Trap:
Free Yourself from the Frustrations that Sabotage Your Life

Les Carter, Ph.D.

Paperback
ISBN: 0-7879-6880-3

"*The Anger Trap* is a masterfully written book, offering penetrating insights into the factors that can imprison individuals in unwanted patterns of frustration. With his well-developed insights and using case examples, Les Carter carefully explains how you can change your thinking, your communication, and your behavior as you release yourself from the ravages of anger gone bad."

—from the Foreword by Frank Minirth, M.D.

"Les Carter has assimilated his years of experience counseling people trapped by anger into a book that I believe will prove helpful to many readers. *The Anger Trap* offers fresh information and understanding that can lead to recovery and reconciliation."

—Zig Ziglar, author and motivational speaker

"The best book on anger out there. Five stars!"

—Dr. Tim Clinton, president, American Association of Christian Counselors

Dr. Les Carter—a nationally recognized expert on the topics of conflict resolution, emotions, and spirituality and coauthor of the best-selling *The Anger Workbook*—has written this practical book that strips away common myths and misconceptions to show viable ways to overcome unhealthy anger and improve relationships. With gentle spiritual wisdom and solid psychological research, Dr. Carter guides you to creating a better, happier life for yourself, your family, and your coworkers.

LES CARTER, PH.D. is the chief resident psychotherapist at the Minirth Clinic, Richardson, Texas, where he has maintained a private counseling practice since 1980. He is a nationally recognized expert on topics including conflict resolution, emotions and spirituality, and marriage and family relationships. Dr. Carter can be reached at www.angerexpert.com

The Anger Workbook for Christian Parents

Les Carter, Ph.D.
and Frank Minirth. M.D.

Paperback
ISBN: 0-7879-6903-6

"Parents will recognize themselves in this book. 'That's me, been there, and said that.' In easily implemented steps, the authors provide insightful, practical suggestions for changing the anger factor in family interactions."

—Dr. Gary L. Landreth, Regents professor and director, Center for Play Therapy, University of North Texas

"Les Carter and Frank Minirth give you all you need to know about how to use this dicey emotion to your advantage so that you become the parent you want to be. As a parent of two boys, I found this resource invaluable, and I know you will too."

—Les Parrott, Ph.D., author, *High-Maintenance Relationships*

In this practical book, anger experts Dr. Les Carter and Dr. Frank Minirth—coauthors of the best-selling book *The Anger Workbook*—show families how to understand and manage anger in order to create harmony at home. Blending biblical wisdom and psychological research, they show how to distinguish between healthy and unhealthy anger and offer proven techniques for dealing with the root causes of anger. Full of real-life examples, checklists, evaluation tools, and study questions, this is a must-have book for those involved with today's youth.

DR. LES CARTER is nationally known psychotherapist at the Minirth Clinic in Richardson, Texas, where he has practiced since 1980.

DR. FRANK MINIRTH is president of the Minirth Clinic, which he founded in 1975.

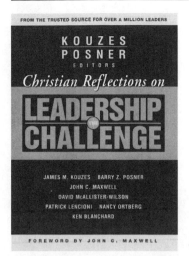

Christian Reflections on the Leadership Challenge

James M. Kouzes
Barry Z. Posner

Hardcover
ISBN: 0-7879-6785-8

". . . facilitates a positive guidance role."
—*Publishers Weekly,* February 9, 2004

Christian Reflections on the Leadership Challenge gathers together in one place a remarkable collection of leaders who share insights on faith and leadership. Well-grounded in research, this reflective and practical book shows how Christian leaders—no matter the setting—put into place The Five Practices of Exemplary Leadership®: Model the Way, Inspire a Shared Vision, Challenge the Process, Enable Others to Act, and Encourage the Heart.

JIM KOUZES and BARRY POSNER are the award-winning coauthors of several best-selling books, including *The Leadership Challenge, Credibility,* and *Encouraging the Heart.* Jim is also an executive fellow at the Center for Innovation and Entrepreneurship at the Leavey School of Business, Santa Clara University, and chairman emeritus of the Tom Peters Company. Barry is the dean of the Leavey School of Business and professor of leadership at Santa Clara University.

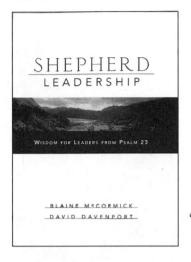

Shepherd Leadership:
Wisdom for Leaders from Psalm 23

Blaine McCormick
David Davenport

Hardcover
ISBN: 0-7879-6633-9

"What a joy to learn that David Davenport has placed his thoughts on paper! He has touched thousands with his teaching—may he and Blaine touch even move through this book."

—Max Lucado, best-selling author and pulpit minister, Oak Hills Church of Christ

"*Shepherd Leadership* is remarkable for showing how timeless truths—from one of the most significant passages in the Bible—apply to the complexities of contemporary organizations. It's abundantly clear that when leaders accept the call to lead like a shepherd, not only is the organizational culture improved but so is the bottom line."

—Ken Blanchard, coauthor, *The One Minute Manager* and *The Servant Leader;* cofounder, Center for FaithWalk Leadership

Psalm 23, the Shepherd's Psalm, provides us with ancient wisdom for today's business leadership challenges—and a lens with which to consider our own leadership as well as the leadership of those around us. It teaches that we can be vigilant without being adversarial, that we can serve without being passive, and that we can guide without commanding. *Shepherd Leadership* offers a visionary new model for transforming leadership practices in business, nonprofit, and religious settings. McCormick and Davenport inspire leaders with a fresh interpretation of this familiar biblical passage, helping all to integrate their spiritual life with their working life through a unique blend of spiritual wisdom and business leadership strategy.

BLAINE MCCORMICK (Waco, TX) is assistant professor of business management at Hankamer School of Business, Baylor University. He is a business consultant, speaker, and the author of two previous books.

DAVID DAVENPORT (Danville, CA) is Distinguished Professor of Public Policy and Law at Pepperdine University. He also serves on a number of corporate and nonprofit boards. David was formerly president of Pepperdine University and president of Starwire, Inc.